MICHIGAN
DAY
TRIPS

BY THEME

by Mike Link

Adventure Publications, Inc.
Cambridge, MN

Dedication

I would like to dedicate the book to Kate, who makes all my travel better.

Acknowledgments

I would like to thank Pure Michigan for the great work they do in publicizing the assets of Michigan. I am also thankful for the great hospitality of the people who live along the shore of Lake Superior and greeted Kate and me as we walked by. Finally, I'd like to thank the Great Lakes themselves, which give Michigan so much of its beauty and deserve better care and protection.

All photos by Mike Link

Cover and book design by Jonathan Norberg

10 9 8 7 6 5 4 3 2 1

Copyright 2013 by Mike Link
Published by Adventure Publications, Inc.
820 Cleveland Street South
Cambridge, MN 55008
1-800-678-7006
www.adventurepublications.net
Printed in China
ISBN: 978-1-59193-268-0

Table of Contents

Traverse City Trail

Michigan is a magnificent place for the outdoor adventurer. Four of the Great Lakes touch the state's borders, so there are unlimited opportunities for sailing, boating, kayaking, canoeing or fishing. But Michigan's outdoor opportunities are not restricted to the Great Lakes, as endless inland adventures await as well. Michigan is ideal for hiking, backpacking and biking. Whatever adventure you choose, Michigan is a state where staying fit is as easy as stepping outside and into nature.

OUTDOOR ADVENTURES

1 Au Sable River

U.S. Forest Service Huron National Forest; Mio Ranger District (989) 826-3252;
Huron Shores Ranger District, Oscoda (989) 739-0728
www.fs.usda.gov/main/hmnf/home

There is nothing like floating down a river, and the Au Sable is world-
class. Recognized as a National Wild and Scenic River, its free-flowing
section is superb and flows through a national forest that is home to
a variety of wildlife, including Kirtland's warbler. The river itself has
trout, bass and walleye. With nearby outfitters who can provide gear
and shuttles and a road paralleling the river, there are many options
for a day trip and for even longer adventures.

2 Bangor/South Haven Heritage Water Trail

PO Box 676, South Haven 49090
www.vbco.org/watertrail.asp

On this water trail, birdsong and greenery will be your constant
companions. Watch for bald eagles, wild turkeys, spotted sandpipers,
great crested flycatchers, and a variety of other species. There are
only 21 miles between Bangor and South Haven, but because of the
lazy current, a trip could turn into a 10-hour paddle—so be sure to
check on water level and currents before setting out. Also, be aware
of overhanging branches and downed trees.

3 Battle Creek Linear Park Pathway

35 Hamblin Ave, Battle Creek 49017; (269) 966-3431
www.bcparks.org/jsps/linear_park.jsp

Battle Creek Linear Park offers unlimited recreational and educational
opportunities. With more than 28 miles of paved pathway, the park is
perfect for a brisk jog or a leisurely stroll. The park is also a resource
for learning more about the world around you, as it features unique
plant, animal, historical and cultural points of interest. Exercise your
body and your mind on the Battle Creek Linear Park Pathway.

4 City of Marquette Bike Path

Marquette
www.mqtcty.org/exploring.html#bike

Marquette's harbor is home to an active marina, a linear park, a lighthouse museum, and a Coast Guard station. There are playgrounds and picnic areas, and the old iron ore dock is like a monument in the water. The brick buildings of the city are on the hill overlooking the marina, and the Victorian mansions are just north of downtown. Presque Isle Park has a nature center and ample areas for playing or a picnic. And the best thing for hikers and bikers is that all of these wonderful landmarks are connected by a 12-mile paved trail. With Lake Superior to cool the area and add to all these wonderful visuals, you can't go wrong.

5 Copper Harbor's Bike Trails

Copper Harbor
www.copperharbortrails.org/

Mountain bikers are a special breed. They do not want flat paved trails and easy routes; they want obstacle-laden trails with mixed grades and plenty of challenges. Copper Harbor features more than 25 miles of forested trails that offer that, and more. If that's not enough, the views will take your breath away (whatever breath you have left after making your way up the steep grades, that is). If anything can match Lake Superior's ruggedness, this is it. For beginners there are three easy trails, but there are trails for intermediate and advanced bikers, too. Trailheads begin at the Copper Harbor Community Building and Keweenaw Mountain Lodge.

6 Falling Waters Trail

1992 Warren Ave, Jackson 49203; (517) 768-2917
www.fallingwatertrail.org/

The Rails-to-Trails Conservancy has found a willing partner in the State of Michigan, and their collaboration has resulted in some of the best biking options in the country. This 10.5-mile trail is just one example of what Michigan has to offer. It follows the railroad bed of the former Michigan Central line, and runners, walkers, in-line skaters and bikers will find an easy and pleasurable route that passes forests, flowers, wetlands, fields and rural landscapes

Before the railroads, this route was a trail used by the Potowatomi Indians. You can take a little side trip to Falling Waters Trail County Park, an area frequented by the Potowatomi.

7 Fred Meijer White Pine Trail State Park

6093 M-115, Cadillac 49601; (231) 775-7911
www.whitepinetrail.com/

At 92 miles, this is the state's longest rail-to-trail conversion and it is paved for over half its length. Like all good trails, this trail can be used for many purposes: for hiking, running and skating in the summer, and skiing and snowmobiling in the winter. The trail itself is a leisurely ride with few slopes and a comforting rural landscape dotted with 10 small towns. This trail was named in honor of Fred Meijer, a benefactor who invested in many trails around the state. Its name also honors the white pine, which is sometimes called the king pine.

8 Hart-Montague Trail State Park

From US 31, exit at Hart Exit (Polk Rd) and go east a quarter mile to the parking lot on the left, Hart 49420; (231) 873-3083
www.michigan.gov/hartmontague

This 22-mile trail was an early addition to Michigan's system of biking trails, which is now envied nationwide. Located in a rural area, this park features charming scenery that includes farms and silos, meadows, birds and flowers, remnant forests, and a combination of scenic overlooks and pleasant towns. Plan to dine in a small-town restaurant, treat yourself to ice cream, and return over the same route; you'll be surprised by how different the return route looks.

9 Hiawatha Water Trail

Big Bay
www.hiawathawatertrail.org

Kayaking on Lake Superior is becoming increasingly popular. A good sea kayak is capable of plying the waves with safety and speed and can get into the lake's hidden coves and bays easier than a canoe. One popular route is the Hiawatha Water Trail, where you can expect to see lighthouses, shipwrecks, and some of the most beautiful rock formations on the lake. This trail will eventually extend from Big Bay to Grand Marais and encompass Pictured Rocks National Lakeshore. The shoreline of the Hiawatha National Forest provides access to this route, as well as a beautiful backdrop. Designated campsites for the water trail provide both a safe haven and access to a good place to set up camp.

10 Huron River Water Trail

Huron River Watershed Council, 1100 N Main St, Ste 210, Ann Arbor 48104; (734) 769-5123
www.huronriverwatertrail.org/

The Huron River flows into Lake Erie, and for 104 miles it connects communities such as Milford, Dexter, Ann Arbor, Ypsilanti and Flat Rock. The consortium of groups and communities that make up the Huron River Water Trail invite you to explore the river, which was frequented by Indians and traders when the valley was wild. With a usually gentle current, the river is worth checking out, but it does have some rocky rapids, so be sure the section you choose to float matches your ability.

11 Huron-Sunrise Trail

292 S Bradley Hwy, Rogers City C of C, Rogers City 49779; (989) 734-2535
www.michigan.org/property/detail.aspx?p=B12644

The Huron-Sunrise Trail spans 10 miles from Rogers City to 40 Mile Point Lighthouse and is the perfect way to discover the beauty of Lake Huron, a Great Lake that gets less recognition and publicity than its more famous neighbors. The trail makes for a nice walk or bike ride, and is a great way to explore the dunes, beaches, streams, parks and hardwood forests of Lake Huron's shoreline. A spur trail leads into the Herman Vogler Conservation Area, which features additional hiking and mountain biking options.

12 Isle Royale National Park

800 E Lakeshore Dr, Houghton 49931-1896; (906) 482-0984
Reduced schedule in May, June and September
www.nps.gov/isro/planyourvisit/outdooractivities.htm

This is one of the least-visited national parks, but that's only because it's one of the most remote and consists almost entirely of wilderness. If you love to hike and/or backpack, this is the place to be. Like Lake Superior that surrounds it, the park is rugged, challenging and rewarding. Hikers can choose loops on either end of the 45-mile-long island or walk from end to end. If you are lucky you may glimpse a moose or a wolf; wolf-moose interactions have been studied on this island since 1958. To reach the island, you need to take a ferry or a plane. Once there, you need to be prepared for a potential delay (on account of the weather). There is a resort at Rock Harbor along with a visitor center and a variety of program options and some supplies. The Windigo

area (on the island's southwest end) has a campground, a visitor center complex, a store, and two rustic rental cabins. Boats leave from Houghton and Copper Harbor, Michigan, and Grand Portage, Minnesota, to carry hikers and explorers; the plane leaves from the Houghton County Airport.

13 Jordan River

Antrim County
www.michigan.gov/dnr/0,4570,7-153-30301_31431_31442-95803--,00.html
www.jvoutfitters.com/Jordan_Valley_Outfitters/Home.html

The 33-mile Jordan River was the first stream designated in the Michigan Natural Rivers Program. From rapids to long lulls, the river offers a variety of conditions and should entertain all paddlers. If you don't have a boat, nearby outfitters are available, and they can also let you know about river conditions and provide shuttle service. By the way, the river is a "world-class" brook trout stream, so bring your fishing gear and don't be in too much of a hurry to reach the end.

14 Kalamazoo River Valley Trail

Kalamazoo; (269) 373-5073
www.kalcounty.com/parks/krvt/

This is another of Michigan's first-rate trails. A work in progress that is constantly being expanded, the 35-plus-mile trail is popular with hikers and bikers alike. Some of the highlights of the trail include Verburg Park, Markin Glen County Park, and the Kalamazoo Nature Center. The cityscape adds interest to the ride and you can take advantage of refreshments and even a little shopping if you want to explore the community as you go.

15 Kal-Haven Bike Trail, Kal-Haven Trail State Park

Bloomingdale
www.michigandnr.com/parksandtrails/details.aspx?id=353&type=SPTR

If you're looking for a long ride, consider combining this trail with the Kalamazoo Trail. This trail is 34.5 miles long and covered with crushed limestone. This surface works fine for road bikes and mountain bikes alike and makes a wonderful hiking path, since it has more give than asphalt. Horses are allowed on 11 miles of the trail and cross-country skiers use it in the winter. The trail covers the distance from South Haven to Kalamazoo; it also features bridges worth seeing, a camel-back bridge, and a covered bridge.

16 Lakeshore Trail

Grand Haven and Holland
www.westmichigantrails.com/LakeshoreTrail.html

Sand dunes, a tunnel of trees, and blue water say it all. This is an inspiring ride, and lake breezes make for a cool ride, even in the middle of summer. Paralleling the Lake Michigan shoreline, this trail connects Grand Haven State Park and Holland State Park, and several other parks are along the route, including Kirk Park, Tunnel Park, and Rosy Mound Natural Area. Each offers a place to rest, picnic and explore. On a hot day, you can cool off by taking a dip in the lake. For a loop ride, connect with Butternut Drive from Holland.

17 Lansing River Trail

Lansing
http://lansingrivertrail.org

A mix of wooden boardwalks and asphalt trail, this is a classic ride along the Red Cedar and Grand Rivers. With a blend of urban and natural scenery, this ride is very popular and riders should be content to stick to a leisurely pace, as this trail can be busy. With possible stops at Potter Park, the University of Michigan arboretums, the Brenke Fish Ladder, the R. E. Olds Transportation Museum, and the historic Turner-Dodge House, there is no limit to how much time you can spend here. The downtown capitol is an additional area you can explore. Hawk Island Park is an excellent spot for picnics and relaxation.

18 Leelanau Trail

Traverse City
http://traversetrails.org/trail/leelanau-trail/

On the Leelanau Trail, you can bike, in-line skate or hike past farms and orchards, as well as through beautiful hardwood forests. In the spring, enjoy the blossoms in the forests and the orchards, and in the summer relax amid the shade and bright red cherries. You can also take a detour from the trail to visit nearby vineyards.

Keep in mind that only half the trail is paved, but the remainder is hard packed and still easy to travel, although it's easier with larger tires. Be sure to return in all seasons, as the autumn leaves are quite a sight.

19 Mackinac Island Biking

Mackinac Island
www.mackinacdirectory.com/mackinac_island/bike_rides.php

This is the only bike trail in the state that is actually a road, and it's a road that doesn't allow cars. You read that right: M-185 doesn't allow cars. It is just you, your bike, and the horses. The road spans 8.2 miles and encircles the island, leading to rest stops, historic points, and great vistas. You might have to ride it twice, once to look inland and the other to look out to the beautiful waters of Lake Huron. Even though the road isn't particularly long, it's recommended that you allow 1–3 hours for the circuit. The only hazards are the "horse apples" that might cause you to zig or zag. For a fee, the ferry to the island will transport your bike, or you can just rent bikes on the island.

20 Manistee River

Huron-Manistee National Forests, 1755 S Mitchell St, Cadillac 49601; (800) 821-6263; U.S. Forest Service, Manistee Ranger District (231) 723-2211; Michigan Department of Natural Resources (231) 775-9727
www.dnr.state.mi.us/publications/pdfs/wildlife/viewingguide/nlp/41Manistee/index.htm
www.fs.usda.gov/recmain/hmnf/recreation

Along with the Au Sable River, the Manistee River serves to cut the L.P. in half. The Manistee flows west to Lake Michigan while the Au Sable flows east to Lake Huron. If you're quiet, you may see a variety of animals, including mink, deer, bears, otters, muskrats and beavers. Mornings and evenings are the best times to spot wildlife. Eagles, ospreys, and herons are common sights, and songbirds love the island and shoreline thickets. The lower Manistee is home to red-shouldered hawks, a species more common in the southern portions of Michigan. Their presence is testimony to the quality of the river woodlands.

21 North Country National Scenic Trail

North Country Trail Association, 229 E Main St, Lowell 49331; (616) 897-5987, (866) 445-3628
http://northcountrytrail.org/

How about a little 4,600-mile hike? That just might exceed a day trip, so how about sampling Michigan's portions of this magnificent national trail? There are many different hiking options, and there are some marvelous sections paralleling Lake Superior, but the trail is not limited to the wilds of the U.P.; in fact, it runs the entire north-south length of the L.P., allowing Michiganders more hiking opportunities on the trail than residents of any other state. Some sections are not complete, but there are more than enough completed sections to satisfy the most dedicated hiker. Sections go through state forests, state parks, national parks, refuges and other public lands, providing ways to discover Michigan by "connecting the dots." Maps and other planning resources for hiking are available at the website.

22 Paint Creek Bike Trail

4393 Collins Rd, Rochester 48306; (248) 651-9260
www.paintcreektrail.org/

In 1983, this Penn Central track was converted to the Paint Creek Trail. Some claim this was the first rail-to-trail conversion, making it a historic ride, but the history is not as important as the ride itself and its forests, fields, wetlands, and its namesake, Paint Creek. Only 8.9 miles long, the ride stretches between Rochester and Lake Orion and makes for an easy there-and-back jaunt, eliminating the need for a shuttle. The limestone surface is 8 feet wide and is open for non-motorized use year-round. This is a very popular trail and one that will immerse you in the peaceful surroundings of nature.

23 Pere Marquette National Wild and Scenic River

Huron-Manistee National Forests, 1755 S Mitchell St, Cadillac 49601;
(800) 821-6263
www.fs.usda.gov/main/hmnf/home
www.fs.usda.gov/recmain/hmnf/recreation
www.rivers.gov/rivers/rivers/pere-marquette.php

Michigan is home to many firsts, but this site is a really significant one for river lovers. The Pere Marquette River was the first river in Michigan to be designated a National Wild and Scenic River. Spring fed, the river begins near Baldwin; it is the longest free-flowing river in the L.P.! Boaters tend to appreciate variety, and this river delivers: its rocky shores, pools and broad marshlands make it an engaging trip. The designated and most scenic portion is the 66-mile stretch from the junction of the Middle and Little South Branches downstream to the Highway 31 Bridge. Unlike the Au Sable and Manistique Rivers, more than 70 percent of the shoreline is privately owned, so be respectful of these property owners.

24 Pere Marquette Rail-Trail

Midland
www.lmb.org/pmrt
www.railstotrails.us/mi_pere_marquette_rail_trail.htm

This trail is a wonderful 30-mile ride between Midland and Clare, where you can stop at the famed Cops & Doughnuts shop. (Note: Confusingly, there is also a Pere Marquette State Trail, but that's a different trail.)

The old CSX rail corridor is popular, and along the route you'll find parking and restrooms, making the journey an enjoyable and convenient trip. But what really catches the imagination is the Tridge—and that's not a misspelling. The Tridge consists of 3 bridges that are connected in the middle. The structure spans the Chippewa and Tittabawassee Rivers, and it's unlike anything else in the state. Described as "one 31-foot central pillar with three spokes," the Tridge might just tempt you to go back and forth until you have crossed all the options.

25 Pictured Rocks National Lakeshore

N8391 Sand Point Rd, PO Box 40, Munising 49862-0040; (906) 387-2607
www.nps.gov/piro/planyourvisit/maritime.htm
www.nps.gov/piro/planyourvisit/scenicsites.htm

Pictured Rocks National Lakeshore is an adventurer's paradise. Known for its spectacular cliffs, vistas and dunes, there are many ways to enjoy the lakeshore. Boat tours give an unparalleled view of the area, but you can also venture on foot, as the trails are well maintained and lead to hidden streams and waterfalls, overlooks, beaches, and even views of shipwrecks. If you can spare the time, a short backpacking trip is the perfect way to enjoy the scenery.

26 Pontiac Lake Recreation Area

7800 Gale Rd, Waterford 48327; (248) 666-1020
www.michigandnr.com/parksandtrails/details.aspx?id=485&type=SPRK

Close to a major city, this recreation area is the perfect place to escape the urban environment and provides opportunities for both exercise and meditation. Consisting of 3,800 acres, there are many adventures to be had here, and there are activities to partake in during each season. Bird watching, horseback riding, biking and hiking are perennial favorites, as is simple relaxation.

27 Porcupine Mountain Wilderness State Park

33303 Headquarters Rd, Ontonagon 49953; (906) 885-5275
www.michigandnr.com/parksandtrails/details.aspx?id=426&type=SPRK

Home to 90 miles of back country trails and 60,000 acres of virgin forest, there are numerous hiking options in this state park. Lake of the Clouds is the most popular destination in the park; set in a deep cleft in the mountain ridges, it is as close to the Scottish Highlands as you can get in the United States.

Keep in mind that this is a wilderness park and even a day trip calls for a more rugged hike. The Lake Superior Trail has many fantastic views of the big lake, but it is 17 miles long and rugged. Pace yourself, or better yet, consider reserving one of their back country cabins and make this more than a simple day trip.

28 Sleeping Bear Dunes National Lakeshore

Philip A. Hart Visitor Center, on M-72, 500 feet east of M-22 in Empire;
(231) 326-5134 ext 328
www.nps.gov/slbe/

The Lake Michigan shoreline is famous for its dunes, and rightfully
so, but the Sleeping Bear Dunes area is truly something special.
Home to a pristine landscape, this is a special place for Odana and
Ojibwa Indians, and it has also inspired generations of Michiganders
and visitors from around the world. Geologically, these are perched
dunes—sand atop an old glacial ridge. Because of that ridge, these
dunes are unusually tall, reaching as high as 400 feet. There are
many ways to appreciate (and have fun on!) the dunes; hiking, dune
climbing and rolling are all options, as are sea kayaking and simple
relaxation. If you love hiking, don't forget to go inland and follow the
trails to bogs, lakes and forested glens.

29 Sylvania Canoe Wilderness

7 miles east of Watersmeet, 39 miles west of Ironwood; (877) 444-6777
www.fs.usda.gov/recarea/ottawa/recarea/?recid=12331

This wilderness area is home to pristine lakes and magnificent
forests and is often compared to the world-famous Boundary Waters
Canoe Area. Those comparisons hold up well. Because this canoe
wilderness is relatively small, you may encounter more canoeists,
but with a little planning you can experience the famous solitude
firsthand. Trips can last from a day to a week or more.

30 Waterloo Recreation Area

16345 McClure Rd, Chelsea 48118; (734) 475-8307
www.michigandnr.com/parksandtrails/details.aspx?id=506&type=SPRK
www.thebig400.com/

Part of The Big 400, this is the largest state park in the L.P., and its
landscape is quite different than that on the U.P. This park is home to
11 inland lakes and 47 miles of hiking trails. Not surprisingly, boating,
swimming, horseback riding, hiking and fishing are all popular pur-
suits. In the winter, cross-country skiing is an option. The ski trails are
ungroomed and skiing can require intermediate to expert skills.

The nearby Phyllis Haehnle Memorial Sanctuary is another reason to visit. From late August to early November, sandhill cranes visit the area. If you want to add education to your visit, the Gerald E. Eddy Discovery Center offers excellent exhibits and programs to help you understand the history of Michigan's geology and natural communities.

31 Yankee Springs Recreation Area

2104 S Briggs Rd, Middleville 49333; (269) 795-9081
www.michigandnr.com/parksandtrails/details.aspx?id=511&type=SPRK

This 5,200-acre recreation area is home to 9 lakes that are replete with camping and fishing options, but don't miss the 30 miles of hiking trails, the 12 miles of mountain biking trails, and 9 miles for horseback riding. In addition, all of these natural areas draw in botanists in spring and summer and bird watchers in spring and fall.

The Powwow at Bay Mills

Long before settlers arrived, Michigan was home to many American Indian peoples, and today many reservations welcome visitors to casinos and campgrounds. The best way to understand Michigan's American Indian tribes and bands is by studying the region's history, learning about American Indian beliefs and traditions, and visiting the museums dedicated to American Indian culture.

AMERICAN INDIAN CULTURE

1 Baraga Monument

US 41, L'Anse 49801
www.exploringthenorth.com/bishopb/shrine.html

It is hard to miss the monument for Father Baraga. This 28-foot-tall statue looks like a giant holding snowshoes, and honors the most famous missionary of Lake Superior. Known as the Snowshoe Priest, he wandered through the wilderness on snowshoes in deep winter and even crossed a stormy Lake Superior in a canoe with a group of Indians. For some, this is a sacred site; for others, it is the story of another non-Indian coming to speak, but not listen. To most of us, it is a fascinating story and an amazing statue. The site is owned by the Missionaries of the Liturgy.

2 Museum of Ojibwa Culture

500 N State St, St. Ignace; (906) 643-9161
http://museumofojibwaculture.net/

This Ojibwa museum is located next to Father Marquette Park, and that is in itself a reflection of the complex history of the American Indian. That history is not a pretty one. American Indians were removed from their land and forced to give up their traditional lifestyle and beliefs. The museum was the location of Marquette's original mission and is also where he is buried.

Outside the museum there are full-size traditional Indian structures, and inside there are exhibits and videos that tell the story of the Ojibwa from their perspective.

3 Powwows

www.500nations.com/Michigan_Events.asp
www.crazycrow.com/Michigan-Powwow.php
www.fallingwatertrail.org/learnmore.htm
http://michiganpowwow.com/
www.umich.edu/~ojibwe/resources/
www.umich.edu/~powwow/
www.walkin-thespirit.com/

The powwow is a combination of a musical festival, a county fair, and a social gathering, and it brings together American Indians from all over. A celebration of American Indian heritage, it is a colorful spectacle with traditional costumes, drum groups, and song.

Non-Indians are invited to attend, and a powwow is a great place to bring children to introduce them to the original inhabitants of the state. Spend time at the powwow, buy some food, explore the reservation, and meet some of the performers.

4 Ziibiwing Center

6650 E Broadway, Mt. Pleasant 48858; (980) 775-4750
www.sagchip.org/ziibiwing/

Three bands of Ojibwa have used their economic gains from gaming to build this museum, which serves as a gathering point and a way to reclaim their heritage and history. It is open to everyone and is an important part of the story of the land we now call Michigan. In these exhibits they share their beliefs and stories in an effort to educate band members and visitors alike. It is important to show respect as you observe and learn. We noticed how important the seasons are for the Ojibwa and how much their movements and activities were dictated by these changing conditions.

Seney Trumpeter Swans

With the Great Lakes blocking the migration flyways, migrating birds need to find a way around the cold water and to the warmer air above the landmasses. As there are only so many paths, these flyways become high-traffic areas, and they are wonderful places to see many birds at once (and for bird counts). Every year, bird watchers venture to these migration hotspots to observe the year's migration.

FOR BIRD WATCHERS & NATURE LOVERS

For Bird
Watchers &
Nature Lovers

1 Binder Park Zoo

400 Division Dr, Battle Creek 49014; (269) 979-1351
www.binderparkzoo.org/

Not all zoos boast vast acreages or immense collections. Sometimes a zoo can blend in with the surrounding community, like Binder Park Zoo does in Battle Creek. With 433 acres of forest and wetland, you can find cool shade on a hot day and natural habitats to explore, such as the wetland "Swamp Adventure." Despite its size, the zoo offers a variety of animals, but feeding the giraffes is the highlight for most visitors. It might be surprising, but the zoo is home to one of the largest giraffe herds in America. The zoo also features a free tram ride and a farm with domestic animals.

2 Bernard W. Baker Sanctuary

21145 15 Mile Rd, Bellevue 49021; (517) 886-9144
www.michiganaudubon.org/conservation/sanctuaries/baker.html

Cranes are revered worldwide, but they are also endangered through-out much of their range. That is no longer true for the sandhill crane, thanks to groups such as the Michigan Audubon Society.

This sanctuary, created in 1941, deserves a share of the applause for a job well done, too. Home to a variety of habitats, there can be as many as 5,000 cranes here, as well as a variety of other birds, includ-ing ospreys, eagles, waterfowl, hawks and marsh birds. With patience (and a good pair of binoculars) you can see many of these species when bird watching. The October Cranefest in the adjacent Kiwanis Youth Area is an excellent event to add to a day at the sanctuary.

3 Detroit River International Wildlife Refuge

Large Lakes Research Station, 9311 Groh Rd, Grosse Ile 48138; (734) 692-7608
www.fws.gov/midwest/detroitriver/

The first wildlife refuges were established under Theodore Roosevelt, due to the growing threat unchecked hunting and commerce posed to wildlife. Today, there are more than 540 refuges. This refuge has the distinction of being the only International Wildlife Refuge in North America. With more than 5,000 acres of marshland on the lower Detroit River and the western shore of Lake Erie, this refuge is located where major flyways—the Atlantic and the Mississippi—converge. If birding isn't your thing, this is also home to a significant walleye population.

4 Detroit Zoo and Belle Isle Nature Zoo

8450 W 10 Mile Rd, Royal Oak 48067; (248) 541-5717
http://detroitzoo.org/
Belle Isle Nature Zoo; (313) 852-4056 ext 3023

With exhibits focusing on Australia, Africa, Asia, the Arctic and Antarctic, plus Amphibiville (a national amphibian conservation center), the Detroit Zoo is on the "A" list. So where do you start when you go to a zoo? Some will walk from front to back, trying to take in everything all at once, while others head to their favorites first and proceed from there.

This zoo is home to aardvarks, zebras and hundreds of species in between. Highlights include the Giraffe Encounter, where you can feed the zoo's tallest creatures, and the lion habitat, where you can get face-to-face with the big cats. If you're lucky, you'll encounter some of the free-roaming wildlife in addition to the captive species in this clean, well-run zoo. For convenience, the Detroit Zoo also operates the Belle Isle Nature Zoo, a smaller display of animals closer to the city. You can visit both zoos or choose the one that is the most convenient for you.

5 GarLyn Zoological Park

W9104 US-2, PO Box 245, Naubinway 49762-0245; (906) 477-1085
www.garlynzoo.com/

In 1994, Gary and Lynn Moore saw their dreams come true when they opened GarLyn Zoological Park. To some, this 10-acre facility is an ark in the wilds of the U.P. Located in the land of dunes and pines, some of the residents were originally pets and part of a private collection of the owners. These animals now serve as greeters and goodwill ambassadors and love a handful of treats from the visitors. Many of the other animals at this zoo were rescued. This is their pleasant recovery retreat, and they can never be released back to the wild. On occasion, local wildlife species will wander in for a visit themselves.

6 Great Lakes Zoological Society

6885 Jackson Rd, Ann Arbor 48103; (734) 332-1628
www.glzszoo.org/

It takes a special group of people to open a zoo that features reptiles, amphibians, insects and birds. Because they're not soft, furry or fuzzy, reptiles, amphibians and insects get a lot of bad PR, and they are hardly the most popular animal species. Even so, they are critical to the life cycle on this planet and they deserve our respect and appreciation.

They have managed to survive for millions of years and now face serious environmental threats. Here you can learn about these underappreciated species and observe things you'd seldom see (or perhaps pass over) at a zoo. The society is staffed by devoted personnel; when you visit, ask them about their species preservation efforts.

7 Huron River Watershed Council— River Roundup and Bug ID Day

Huron River Watershed Council, 1100 N Main St, Ste 210, Ann Arbor 48104; (734) 769-5123
www.hrwc.org/volunteer/roundup

Roll up your sleeves and dig in. Get down, get your hands dirty, and be a scientist. To determine the health of the Huron River, Watershed Council representatives will be turning over rocks and catching critters you probably didn't even know lived there. These little insects live in the water, and their ability to survive depends on water quality. If water quality is poor, you will find fewer mayflies, stoneflies and caddisflies. Doing this River Roundup makes you the scientist, and the species you collect will help scientists determine the health of the stream.

8 Keweenaw Migratory Bird Festival

520 Shelden Ave, Houghton 49931; (906) 523-4612
www.keweenawimbd.org/festival.html

The Keweenaw Migratory Bird Festival doesn't occur on only one day; it lasts the entire month of May. Because of weather conditions, some days might be worse than others for bird watching, but on those days you can always enjoy the lake and the rugged scenery of Brockway Mountain. If you visit, be sure to look for hawks. This is an important hawk migration route and 17 species have been sighted here. This mountain observatory also has smaller lakes, beaches, bogs and forests where a variety of migrating species can be found, so grab a checklist and see which species you can spot. Also, before you go, check the schedule and plan your trip to coincide with one of the many excellent speakers during the month.

9 Kirtland's Warbler Tours

Tours offered at two locations, May 15–June 4: 107 McKinley Rd, Mio 48647; (989) 826-3252; 2650 I-75 Business Loop, Grayling Ramada Inn, Grayling 49738; Hotel (800) 292-9055; Tour (517) 641-4277; www.fws.gov/midwest/endangered/birds/Kirtland/ www.fs.usda.gov/detail/hmnf/passes-permits/?cid=STELPRDB5247524 www.michiganaudubon.org/kirtlandswarbler.html

Sometimes just a bit of birdsong coming through an open car window is enough to signal that you're about to observe one of the rarest warblers in the world. In 1987, there were only 167 male Kirtland's warblers living in the jack pine forest, and they represented the worldwide population. Then, ornithologists and foresters joined forces and took action. Because of these human allies, this bluish gray and yellow warbler is now a success story that you can see for yourself on either of the two guided tours offered.

10 Lake Bluff Bird Sanctuary

2890 Lakeshore Rd, Manistee 49660; (231) 723-4042 www.michiganaudubon.org/conservation/sanctuaries/bluff.html

Michigan Audubon strives to connect birds and people for the benefit of both through efforts in research, education and conservation. It has done just that at the Lake Bluff Bird Sanctuary. The sanctuary boasts more than 1,500 feet of Lake Michigan beach frontage and more than 2 miles of preserved and maintained trails on its 76 acres. Originally landscaped as an arboretum, many notable specimens have been preserved, such as a California redwood, a ginkgo tree, a giant sequoia, a sycamore tree, and many large cottonwood trees. Also notable are 170-plus bird species, both nesting and migrating through the area, such as bald eagles, rare and common shorebirds, and migrating warblers. This sanctuary is the result of a gift from a Michigan family and is now home to a quaint bed & breakfast. The sanctuary offers month-

ly guided hikes and hosts the Chickadee Christmas open house in December. Manistee Audubon meets on the second Wednesday of the month.

11 Leslie Science & Nature Center

1831 Traver Rd, Ann Arbor 48105; (734) 997-1553; http://lesliesnc.org/

We may not think about it often, but animals are injured all the time, often because of human activities or development. But animals can't make a 911 call when they need help. Luckily, the Leslie family helped create a center where some of these injured animals can get care. Because the center deals with animals with serious injuries, the animals end up being permanent residents. In the process, they help us learn about them. The animals get a good deal, too: they are well cared for and are acclimated to people and get to serve as ambassadors for their relatives in the wild. The center is home to many birds of prey, as well as a "critter house" that is home to a variety of resident mammals, reptiles and amphibians. The center's animals aren't just on display; they also participate in educational programming. Check the animals out and then go for a walk on the trail to celebrate their healthy relatives out in the wild.

12 Millie Mine Bat Cave

Iron Mountain 49801; (906) 774-8530
www.dnr.state.mi.us/publications/pdfs/wildlife/viewingguide/up/07Bat/index.htm

We know—bats are not the most popular animals. But ask a person in the midst of mosquito season if they'd like something to prey upon those lovely little bloodsuckers, and the bat may suddenly become more popular. And in some places, bats *are* popular; perhaps you've heard of the thousands of people who line up in Austin, Texas, to watch bats take their nightly flight, or the people who gather at Mammoth Cave just to see bats. But who would think that you could come to a mine shaft and find a breeding colony of 50,000 bats, 360 feet down? There are actually about 30 similar sites in the U.P., but this site features naturalists who help you interpret what you're seeing. The bats emerge from hibernation in April and May, and they prepare for winter in September and October. Whenever you visit, you will be impressed.

13 Oden State Fish Hatchery

8258 S Ayr Rd, Alanson 49764; (231) 348-0998
www.michigan.gov/dnr/0,4570,7-153-10364_28277-22423--,00.html

Whether it takes place in streams, in small inland lakes, or in the Great Lakes, fishing is popular throughout Michigan, and the state fish hatcheries are kept busy supporting this highly popular form of recreation. Fortunately, they have chosen to share the hatchery experience with visitors. Visitors are treated to a variety of attractions: hiking trails, exhibits, signs, and even fish ponds where you can feed the lunkers. We especially liked seeing the train car that once transported fish from the hatchery to the lakes—imagine the fish stories the fish got from that. When we visited, a number of children were enjoying watching brown, rainbow and brook trout via a clear window built along the side of a natural stream. In the fish pond, there are some true lunkers and you can feed them pellets that the hatchery provides. Seeing them swirl below your feet is not the same as feeling them on the line, but it's breathtaking all the same.

14 Pointe Mouillee State Game Area

37205 Mouillee Rd, Route 2, Rockwood 48173; (734) 379-9692
www.dnr.state.mi.us/publications/pdfs/wildlife/viewingguide/slp/107Mouillee/
index.htm
www.lre.usace.army.mil/newsandevents/publications/publications/pointemouillee-beneficialuse/
http://miwaterfowlfest.org/

When it comes to ducks, some fans of these birds bring along binoculars, while others bring hunting gear. Whatever their equipment, both groups love waterfowl. At Pointe Mouillee, the Huron River enters Lake Erie, and during migration, its 4,040 acres of restored marshland serve as a temporary home to thousands of waterfowl, shorebirds, wading birds, and birds of prey. Late summer and early fall are the peak times for the magnificent concentration. In September there is a Waterfowl Festival that can help you get the most out of your visit. Pointe Mouilee is one of the largest freshwater marsh restoration projects in North America.

15 Potter Park Zoo

1301 S Pennsylvania Ave, Lansing 48912; (517) 483-4222
www.potterparkzoo.org/

Located along the river corridor and biking and walking trails, the Potter Park Zoo is not far from the state capitol. Though not large, the zoo is big enough for an excellent experience. They zoo features some rare animals, such as Amur tigers and a snow leopard; this is a far cry from

the park's early days, back in 1920, when a group of elk were moved to the park and became the first zoo residents. Now the zoo boasts a new wolf exhibit, river otter and Arctic fox displays, and a 400-bird interactive aviary. If you bring children with you, the Farmyard Adventures area is a good choice, as it features miniature pigs.

16 Seney National Wildlife Refuge

1674 Refuge Entrance Rd, Seney 49883; (906) 586-9851
www.fws.gov/midwest/seney/

This is one of the great wildlife refuges. When you visit, you'll be greeted by swans, scolded by geese, and have a chance to see a wide variety of other wildlife. The wetlands and forests in this area were once known as the Great Manistique Swamp and, like many wetlands and forests of the Midwest, they have a history of being significantly altered by humans. Despite the alterations, the refuge has a rich mosaic of habitats and ecosystems, managed for an array of ecological conditions that benefit a variety of wildlife such as beavers, ducks, loons, turtles, otters, bears, sandhill cranes, wolves, snowshoe hares, warblers, etc. Many of these species can be spotted along the 7-mile-long Marshland Wildlife Drive; the more adventurous may want to consider bicycling the back roads, hiking the ski trails or paddling the Manistique River. Before venturing out onto the refuge, check out the visitor center, open 7 days a week mid-May through mid-October, for more information and tips on what to look for.

17 Shiawassee National Wildlife Refuge

6975 Mower Rd, Saginaw 48601; (989) 777-5930
www.fws.gov/midwest/Shiawassee/

The American Bird Conservancy has designated this refuge as an Important Bird Area because of the significant number of migratory geese, ducks, shorebirds and songbirds that pass through each year. Birds use this as a staging area, and that's a concept that many people neglect to think about. When protecting bird habitat, one can't protect only the birds' winter and summer areas. That leaves out the areas necessary for resting and refueling; the equivalent of having gas stations only at the ends of a freeway. Thankfully, this area was protected; the Wildlife Drive along the Shiawassee River is designed to help you spot as many species as possible.

18 Tawas Point Birding Festival

6011 W St. Joseph Hwy, Lansing 48917; (517) 886-9144
http://tawasbirdfest.com/

Become a birder! It doesn't matter if you've been filling your bird feeders for a lifetime and keeping a lifelist, or if you're just now deciding to see what birding is all about: this Birding Festival is a wonderful place to begin. Here you can catch workshops, go on field trips with experienced and enthusiastic people, and learn about birding. With the scenery of Tuttle Marsh, Clark's Marsh, and Tawas Point and its classic lighthouse, you will not only be observing birds, but enjoying beautiful landscapes. The festival takes place in May, when warblers are likely to add color and motion to the event. Keep your binoculars handy; more than 170 species have been recorded here!

19 Tuttle Marsh Wildlife Area

Huron-Manistee National Forests, Old US 23 & Tuttle Marsh Rd, Oscoda 48750; (989) 739-0728
www.n-sport.com/TuttleMarshWildlifeArea.html

Wetlands were once drained in an effort to eliminate them from rural lands, but today we realize how diverse and species-intense these places can be. Today, ditches and water controls are used to maintain water quality, and this has resulted is an enrichment of the groundwater, and a paradise for waterfowl, mammals and amphibians. A drive through this wildlife area will allow you to observe osprey nests, sandhill cranes, a great blue heron rookery, and shorebirds on the mudflats. Waterfowl can be abundant and elusive birds, such as rails and bitterns, and hide in the vegetation, so you can only hear their calls. If you are lucky, maybe you'll catch a quick, satisfying glance of a black bear or a bobcat.

20 Whitefish Point Bird Observatory

Visitor Center: 18330 N Whitefish Point Rd, Paradise 49768; (906) 492-3596
Mailing Address: 16914 N Whitefish Point Rd, Paradise 49768
http://wpbo.org/

Whitefish Point is the third-largest peninsula on Lake Superior's south shore and the shortest distance across the lake to Canada, at 19 miles. Because of this geography, Whitefish Point sees a large concentration of hawks, falcons, eagles and owls during spring migration. An average of 20,000 raptors fly through the area as Whitefish Point Bird Observatory

(WPBO) continues its 30-plus years of migration research. The Spring Fling, held during the last weekend in April, is WPBO's annual migration celebration and the official opening of the Owl's Roost interpretive center and gift shop. In the summer, the Point becomes home to the endangered piping plover. These shorebirds nest along the sandy cobblestone beach. Another summer visitor is the juvenile northern saw-whet owl. Recently hatched, these owls pass through in the hundreds in July and August. During the spring, summer and fall, WPBO conducts nightly owl banding for these and the eight other species of owls that can be found. Autumn brings our largest concentration of waterfowl and shorebirds. With a seasonal average of 80,000 waterbirds, loons, grebes, ducks, mergansers and geese follow the Lake Superior shoreline on their way to the Gulf Coast or Atlantic coastline. The fall also brings an end to another year of migration data collection. Because of this phenomenal flyway, WPBO is designated a Globally Important Bird Area by the American Bird Conservancy. Whitefish Point is truly a birding paradise.

21 W. K. Kellogg Bird Sanctuary

12685 E C Ave, Augusta 49012; (269) 671-2510
www.kbs.msu.edu/visit/birdsanctuary

Okay, we know that people complain that there are too many geese on lawns and in parks, but that wasn't always the case. Last century, the goose population suffered and was reduced to a critical level, and this bird sanctuary was part of the recovery. Today, trumpeter swans are trying to make a comeback and once again this sanctuary is trying to do its part. But those large birds are not the only benefactors. When habitat is maintained, many species succeed, and this is a place to enjoy natural abundance, along with grouse, pheasants and quail in the upland game bird display area. In addition to all the wild birds, there are captive birds of prey on display, such as a bald eagle, red-tailed hawks, an eastern screech-owl, and more. A three-quarter-mile paved trail passes by Wintergreen Lake and connects both areas.

Meijer Sculpture and Garden

Maybe it's the inspiration of the Great Lakes or the beauty of the wild inland forests, but Michigan is blessed with an abundance of art. Ranging from small-town museums and outdoor sculpture parks to major exhibits at more traditional museums, almost wherever you turn in Michigan, you'll find the fine arts.

THE FINE ARTS

1 AACTMAD—Ann Arbor Community of Traditional Music and Dance

4531 Concourse Dr, Ann Arbor 48108
www.aactmad.org/

Dance is a part of almost every culture, and many ethnic groups and cultures have their own specific kind of dances. Familiar examples include Morris dance, Celtic dance, and contra dance. Hosting more than 200 events every year, this organization seeks to popularize traditional music and dance. Join them for Dancing in the Streets on Labor Day, or the Dawn Dance Weekend, Saturday night contra dances, or English and American dance. Or you can simply choose between square dance and swing; there are just so many great options here. Most of the dances emphasize community and welcome beginners, with or without a partner. Generally, all dances are taught or walked through before the music starts.

2 Ann Arbor Folk Festival

University of Michigan, Hill Auditorium, 825 N University Ave, Ann Arbor 48109
The Ark, 316 S Main St, Ann Arbor 48104; (734) 761-1800
Calls answered 9 a.m. til 5 p.m. M–F
www.theark.org/

The Ann Arbor Folk Festival, held during the last weekend in January, is a traditionally rootsy music celebration with more than three decades of performances. Presented by The Ark, the celebration is also an attempt to preserve our musical heritage and to share it with new audiences, as well as established listeners. The Ark is more than four decades old and was created by area churches as a place where people could gather. The fact that a nonprofit music venue can last that long is a testament to the quality of the project and the people who run it. If you can't make the festival, The Ark is a year-round, 400-seat music venue with outstanding performances from new and established artists. Check out their calendar on the website.

3 Detroit Institute of Arts

5200 Woodward Ave, Detroit 48202; (313) 833-7900
www.dia.org/

This art collection is exhaustive and can be exhausting if you try to take it all in with one visit. Designed by Paul Cret, the museum building was referred to as the "temple of art" as soon as it opened, and that title is still appropriate. The museum boasts that its collection is "one of the top six in the United States"; to us, the top attraction was the Diego Rivera mural which dominates the walls in the center court. This huge mural is a reflection on the industry and working people of Detroit; it is massive, colorful and it's worth taking a trip to Detroit just to stand in its midst and slowly turn in a circle to take it all in. The collection also features old masters like Van Gogh and other international art, as well as American Indian artwork.

4 East Lansing Art Festival (ELAF)

410 Abbot Rd, #202, East Lansing 48823; (517) 319-6804
www.elartfest.com/

The East Lansing Art Festival is held in downtown East Lansing and is often listed as one of the top 100 fine art festivals in the nation. Taking place in the spring, this free event blends juried fine art and craft exhibits with music, children's activities, and an international food court. If you go, wander over to the Michigan State University campus and add their Spring Arts and Crafts Show to your weekend fun.

5 Ella Sharp Museum of Art & History

3225 Fourth St, Jackson 49203; (517) 787-2320
www.ellasharp.org/

This small museum campus features a unique combination of art and history. The centerpiece of the museum is the nineteenth-century farmhouse, but the museum is also home to several galleries, exhibits pertaining to Jackson's history and shops and other historic buildings. The one-room schoolhouse is fun, but it is not part of the art exhibit, nor is the woodworking shop, doctor's office or the general store. An interesting option is the restaurant in Ella's Granary. For us, the highlight was the Wildlife Art exhibit, which seems appropriate based on the woodsy museum setting.

6 Frederik Meijer Garden & Sculpture Park

1000 E Beltline Ave NE, Grand Rapids 49525; (888) 957-1580, (616) 957-1580
www.meijergardens.org/

One day is just not enough to really see and enjoy all this park has to offer. You can rush through, but art isn't (or shouldn't) be about rushing around in order to check items off a list. What we really liked was the interplay between nature and art—nature was valued for its artistic contributions as much as the sculptures. Whether it was the outside gardens, the indoor floral displays, or the natural wetlands and forest, the natural scenery made this a full, rich experience. There is also a Children's Garden that combines art and play. If you are not sure you really like art, this is the place to visit. There is so much to engage with, you might just find that art becomes a subtle and exciting part of your own experience.

7 Gilmore International Keyboard Festival

Irving S. Gilmore International Keyboard Festival, 359 S Kalamazoo Mall, Ste 101, Kalamazoo 49007; (269) 342-1166
http://gilmorekeyboardfestival.org/

Since 1989, this biennial piano festival has brought the best keyboard artists to Kalamazoo. In honor of a local businessman, this nationally prominent festival has contests and awards in classical, jazz, chamber, and other forms of music. There is also an emphasis on young and promising artists. There is a Rising Stars performance series, as well as a Piano Masters Series, both of which offer concerts to the public. Check the website or give them a call to find out when the next festival is being held.

8 Grand Rapids Art Museum

101 Monroe Ctr, Grand Rapids 49503; (616) 831-1000
www.artmuseumgr.org/

In Grand Rapids, one of the most prominent artistic statements is Alexander Calder's famous sculpture *La Grande Vitesse* in the downtown area. The museum gained prominence by hosting loan exhibits of international works, but the collection and exhibits needed a new building that could properly display their collection.

This led to the creation of the new exhibit hall, a modern building that, perhaps most importantly, is a LEED-certified building. This means that this beautiful building is also energy efficient, dispelling the notion that environmentally sensitive design cannot be interesting and appealing. The art here is just as significant as the building, with masters like Dürer, Rembrandt, Homer and Warhol.

9 Hiawatha Traditional Music Festival

At the Marquette Tourist Park, PO Box 414, Marquette 49855; (906) 226-8575
http://hiawathamusic.org/

An event with a history of more than three decades of performance and entertainment, the Hiawatha Music Co-Op supports a 3-day festival of traditional American acoustic music and traditional dance. Drawing an audience from throughout the U.P. and across the country, the festival features a variety of musical styles, including Cajun and Celtic, as well as folk and blues. These performers are often world-class musicians, and if you are an artist or a fan, you might like the "meet-the-artist" sessions or the musical instruction that is part of the festival schedule.

10 Interlochen Center for the Arts

4000 M-137, Interlochen 49643; (231) 276-7200 www.interlochen.org/

If you walk on campus during one of the Interlochen Center's open houses, the saying "there's music in the air" will be a reality. As you walk from studio to studio and hear the different forms of music being played by the students, you'll be inspired, and that's just one of the options for the visitor. In addition to the students, there are guest artists, lecturers and exhibits that enrich the overall art experience. If you are in the area without time to stop, you can tune in to their performances on public radio.

11 Kalamazoo Institute of Art

314 S Park St, Kalamazoo 49007; (269) 349-7775
www.kiarts.org/

While the Kalamazoo Institute of Art provides access to a great world of art, one of the premiere events it holds is the Kalamazoo Art Fair. Held on the first weekend of June, local artists exhibit their creations, making for a fun start to summer. The museum also hosts an art school that ensures local art will have a promising future. Because its exhibits are temporary, there is always something new to see. If you come on a Tuesday, take an ARTbreak and check out the speakers or artists at noon. The museum also hosts jazz concerts on Fridays from 5:30–7:30 p.m.

12 Krasl Art Center

707 Lake Blvd, St. Joseph 49085; (269) 983-0271
www.krasl.org/exhibits_collections.php

Every great museum has a trademark exhibit, something that sets it apart from other museums, something besides a different painting by the same artist who is found in all the other museums. The Krasl Art Center has set itself apart by collecting contemporary sculpture. That does not mean they do not have other art forms, but their sculpture collection has led to a national reputation. Contemporary art is wide-ranging in style and might differ from what you might expect to see at a museum. The museum also includes an art lab, which they describe as "a venue for all artists who are pushing the boundaries of medium and form." Try to schedule your visit when the Krasl Art Fair on the Bluff is being held; *Sunshine Artist* magazine named it one of the best art fairs in the nation.

13 Marshall M. Fredericks Sculpture and Garden Museum

7400 Bay Rd, University Center 48710; (989) 964-7125
http://marshallfredericks.org/

After visiting this museum, we began to see how prevalent Marshall M. Fredericks (1908–98) sculpture is throughout Michigan. Once we recognized his style, we soon noticed it all over the place. As we drove by parks and buildings we would see one and say, "There's another Fredericks." The distinct style and clean, uncomplicated lines of his sculptures convey a story, and often bring a smile. For us, that is terrific art. This museum features more than 200 works by Marshall M. Fredericks, the Michigan sculptor who developed an international reputation. We loved seeing how the art was created, comparing the different samples, and then walking around outdoors in the sculpture garden, where they are really at home. This museum and the sculpture garden are located within the campus of Saginaw Valley State University.

14 Michigan Legacy Art Park

12500 Crystal Mountain Dr, Thompsonville 49683; (231) 378-4963
www.michlegacyartpark.org/

The theme of this art park is "Where Art, Nature and History Meet." Complete with a wooded preserve, fresh air, hiking trails, and more than 40 sculptures that depict the history of Michigan, this is an inspiring place. In addition to the sculptures, there are 30 poetry stones along the pathways. To discover what is here, pick up a trail map at the visitor service center. Take along a picnic, hike the trails and then talk about the history depicted around you; it might just give you a greater appreciation of the state.

15 Motown Museum

2648 W Grand Blvd, Detroit 48208; (313) 875-2264
www.motownmuseum.com
www.motownmuseum.com/mtmpages/

For anyone born into the Rock and Roll era, this is an icon of music and art. Motown Records was a small place that made big hits. Berry Gordy Jr. christened an obscure little house in Detroit "Hitsville, U.S.A." and it resulted in some of the most memorable songs, artists and performances in entertainment history. At the Motown Museum there are photographs and memorabilia that tell the story, but it is the music that will make the connection for you, and with artists like Smokey Robinson and the Miracles, Martha and the Vandellas, The Four Tops, Jackson 5, and The Supremes, there are many connections to be made. And the most amazing fact is that the bands listed above are just a sampling of what Hitsville has produced.

16 Museum of Contemporary Art Detroit

4454 Woodward Ave, Detroit 48201; (313) 832-6622
www.mocadetroit.org/about.html

Bringing contemporary art to the art-loving public is a big task. Forms and formats change over time and the general public is not always up-to-date when it comes to the newest art movements. So when you visit, test your open-mindedness and explore the new forms without comparing them to the old. Even the gift store items here differ from the traditional art museums and this makes the visit exciting. Let yourself be shocked, moved and challenged.

17 Pewabic Pottery National Historic Landmark

Pewabic Pottery, 10125 E Jefferson Ave, Detroit 48214; (313) 626-2000
www.pewabic.org/

Dating back to 1903, this national landmark has a long history, and to this day it boasts a tradition of craftmanship that is reflected in the works it produces. On the first floor, you can visit the gift shop; the second floor is home to a museum, studios and galleries.

Pewabic Pottery vessels and tiles continue to be collector's items, and each is unique in color and design. Once you see the products, you will begin to recognize their creations in buildings around the state and in a variety of art collections. In addition, heirloom architectural styles are made here and are ordered from all over the world. There are many ways to take part in the revival of an art form that has become rare: tour, shop or take an education class and learn how to make your own pottery.

18 Saugatuck Center for the Arts

400 Culver St, PO Box 940, Saugatuck 49453; (269) 857-2399
www.sc4a.org/

The Saugatuck Center for the Arts offers year-round programming inside a renovated pie factory. This is a place for creativity, with classes, workshops, art exhibitions, a professional Equity summer theatre, and performances featuring Grammy Award-winning performers. Music, theatre and film in an intimate 410-seat theatre make this the place to be, and it attracts guests from around the country. The energy here is sure to inspire. As an art venue, what more could you want? While the building no longer features factory-produced pies, good food is still celebrated with a summer Green Market and other food-related events throughout the year.

19 University of Michigan Museum of Art

525 S State St, Ann Arbor 48109-1354; (734) 764-0395
www.umma.umich.edu/

Universities have played an important role in educating new artists and investing in the world of art. Following that tradition, this museum underwent a major expansion in 2009 and has helped the museum to live up to its mission "to bridge visual art and contemporary culture, scholarship and accessibility, tradition and innovation." They like to think of their museum as a "'town square' for the twenty-first century." With an art collection that dates back to the 1850s and access to the expansive world of contemporary art, this a perfect blend of old and new.

The Fine Arts

Lake Superior

Beaches might make you think of the Caribbean or the Florida or California coasts, but those places have nothing on Michigan. Surrounded by Lakes Michigan, Superior, Huron and Erie, and with more than 11,000 inland lakes and a myriad of rivers and streams, Michigan has more freshwater shoreline than any other state in the country. If that does not motivate you to put on your swimsuit, grab the sunscreen, and head for the beach, then it must be winter.

BEACHES & DUNES

1 Aloha State Park

4347 Third St, Cheboygan 49721; (231) 625-2522
www.michigandnr.com/parksandtrails/Details.aspx?id=434&type=SPRK

This park is not Hawaii, but in the summer who needs it to be? Located on Mullett Lake, there is a boat launch, campsites, and the park is only a short distance from the Straits of Mackinac and Lake Huron. The lake is perfect for swimming; it has a sandy bottom and features a nice gradual slope leading to deep water. Let us put it this way—Aloha State Park is a summer destination. A word of warning: if you want to camp here, it's so popular you must reserve a site at least 6 months in advance.

2 Gillette Sand Dune Visitor Center

6585 Lake Harbor Rd, P. J. Hoffmaster State Park, Muskegon 49441; (231) 798-3573
www.michigan.gov/dnr/0,1607,7-153-10369_46675_58086---,00.html

Located in P. J. Hoffmaster State Park, this center helps visitors understand sand dunes, which are as complex as they are beautiful. The center is centered atop a large sand dune, a perfect place to observe and appreciate the dunes. In addition, the center's excellent exhibits help visitors learn about dune ecology and just how fragile dunes really are (despite how strong and stable they may seem). The exhibits include dioramas, animations about dune formation, and many learning stations.

3 Holland State Park

2215 Ottawa Beach Rd, Holland 49424; (616) 399-9390
www.michigandnr.com/parksandtrails/Details.aspx?id=458&type=SPRK

This is not the place to find tulips, but the sunsets here are just as colorful and a perfect complement to Lake Michigan to the west. Sailboats often dot the blue water and add to the picturesque setting, but the beach is still the main attraction. Even if the weather changes, there's much to do, thanks to the campgrounds, picnic shelter, and even a rustic lodge. We highly recommend the dune boardwalk. Because it is highly elevated, it makes it easy to observe the lake and the dunes.

4 Ludington State Park

8800 W M-116, Ludington 49431; (231) 843-2423
www.michigandnr.com/parksandtrails/details.aspx?id=468&type=SPRK
www.visitludington.com/statepark/

Boasting a picturesque beachfront (as well as many popular regional and local beaches), this park is also home to some special features. If the waters of Lake Michigan are too rough or cold, you can swim at Hamlin Lake Beach; the lake itself is also part of a well-known canoe trail. If it's hiking you're interested in, there are 18 miles of trails. This is also a park that lends itself well to photography, so bring your camera. The beach itself is perfect for beach volleyball, and there is plenty of room for your best sand castle. If this is a family event, there should be more than enough to do to satisfy everyone—from the beach bum to the angler.

5 Oval Beach

698 Water St, Saugatuck
Saugatuck-Douglas Visitors Bureau, 2902 Blue Star Hwy, Douglas 49406
(269) 857-1701
www.saugatuck.com/beaches.asp

Everyone wants a Condé Nast rating and Oval beach got theirs: it was dubbed one of the top 25 shorelines by Condé Nast's *Traveler Magazine*, and MTV named it one of the top five beaches in the country. *National Geographic Traveler* named it one of the top two freshwater beaches in the United States and the *Chicago Tribune* ranked it the number one beach on Lake Michigan. After endorsements like that, what can you do but see it for yourself? The beach has a lot going for it: its soft sand is vaunted and it's easy to access, plus the convenient concession stands make it easy to grab a snack. Others love the sunset—where on this coast is there *not* a great sunset? Keep in mind that given this beach's popularity, you'll encounter people, but if you're looking for solitude, all you have to do is walk north several hundred yards to a more secluded spot. The beach is a mile long and practically deserted on the north end.

6 Petoskey Beach State Park

2475 M-119, Petoskey 49770; (231) 347-2311
www.michigandnr.com/parksandtrails/Details.aspx?id=483&type=SPRK

Little Traverse Bay is famous for its quaint coastal communities, but the beauty of the bay is why they are here. Enjoy the western expanse of the bay from Petoskey Beach State Park and catch a sunset or two. Perfect for painters, collectors of Petoskey stones (see pages 122 and 126), swimming, or sunbathing, this is a convenient park for locals and

Beaches & Dunes

tourists alike. Even before you sit down to enjoy the sunset, you can enjoy the varying colors of the bay. If you want to take a bike ride, a trail connects the park to the town of Petoskey.

7 Pictured Rocks National Lakeshore

PO Box 40, Munising 49862-0040
Interagency Visitor Center (year-round), 400 E Munising Ave, Munising 49862; (906) 387-3700
Grand Sable Visitor Center (summer only), E21090 Co Rd H-58, Grand Marais; (906) 494-2660
www.nps.gov/piro/

Pictured Rocks National Lakeshore is included in several different sections of this book, and for good reason: there is simply so much to see and do there. The beaches are just one reason to visit. Walking the rugged Twelvemile Beach is a pleasure. Whether it is the breeze and waves, the shorebirds, or signs of old shipwrecks, this beach is pristine and protected. If the word "unspoiled" was ever appropriate for a beach, this is it. There is also a long beach beneath the Grand Sable Dunes, and high, perched bluffs. Surprisingly, this beach is rocky and a wonderful place to look at beach cobbles. Within Pictured Rocks National Lakeshore, removing rocks or other natural features is prohibited.

8 Port Crescent

1775 Port Austin Rd, Port Austin 48467; (989) 738-8663
www.michigandnr.com/parksandtrails/Details.aspx?id=486&type=SPRK

Lake Huron has beaches to match Lakes Michigan and Superior. With 3 miles of sand beach on the sheltered Saginaw Bay, this is a popular place. In addition to the shallow waters and sandy shore, there are opportunities for fishing, canoeing, hiking, cross-country skiing, birding and hunting. If you or your family desire more sand and sun, there is a boardwalk, a visitor center, and lots of scenic views to find and enjoy.

9 Redwyn Dunes Nature Sanctuary

M-26, Eagle Harbor 49950; (800) 338-7982
www.michigannature.org/home/sancts/redwyn/redwyn.shtml

This place is something different. This isn't designed for recreation, but as a sanctuary where you can sincerely contemplate and interact with nature. Here you can relax and take in the mile-long trail, the stable dunes, and the woods of red oak and pine. If you go, bring a camera or your art supplies, write in a journal or be a naturalist.

10 Silver Lake Sand Dunes and State Park

9679 W State Park Rd, Mears 49436; (231) 873-3083
www.michigandnr.com/parksandtrails/Details.aspx?id=493&type=SPRK

In this book, we often emphasize trips that offer quiet and solitude, but this site is the exception. This 2,000-acre sand area allows off-road drivers to test their skills amid deep sand, and there are also jeep rentals and dune rides available. But not all the dunes are open to off-road drivers. The park is divided into several sections. The center portion of the park is reserved for hiking, walking and simple beach activities. The north area is open for dune rides, and the southern portion is the home of Mac Wood's Dune Rides, which has been in existence for more than 80 years.

11 Sleeping Bear Dunes National Lakeshore

9922 Front St, Empire 49630; (231) 326-5134
www.nps.gov/slbe/

How can you go wrong with the place that was voted the "Most Beautiful Place in America" by the viewers of *Good Morning America*? With more than 31 miles of pristine beach, the huge perched dunes, and the deep blue waters of Lake Michigan, this is a summer paradise. With so many trails to explore, park facilities, and even inland lakes, this place is a must-visit. And if these beaches are not remote and peaceful enough for you, there are miles more of beaches on two islands that are part of the national lakeshore.

12 South Haven Beaches

Water St, South Haven 49090; (269) 637-0726.
http://south-haven.com/pages/beaches/beaches.html

There are seven beaches to choose from; yes, you read right—seven! The beaches on the northern and southern ends seem to be the largest (and busiest), and they include concession stands, parking and rest-rooms. You can also play volleyball, have a picnic, set up your grill or just relax. Packard Beach offers similar options, while others specialize in sunsets and sand only. The young at heart will also find a skateboard park at South Haven and a pier that invites you to take an evening stroll. Like at all the dunes and beaches, there are myriad options if you choose to leave the sand, walk, explore and get exercise.

13 Van Buren State Park

23960 Ruggles Rd, South Haven 49090; (269) 637-2788
www.michigandnr.com/parksandtrails/Details.aspx?id=502&type=SPRK

Not far from South Haven and its many beaches, this small state park has high dunes, a campground, and offers picnicking, hiking, biking, skiing and snowmobiling in addition to beach options. A state trail passes through the park and is perfect for hiking and biking. The beach here is not particularly large, but a great place to relax, and one that is still close to the shops and excitement of South Haven's tourist area.

14 Warren Dunes State Park

12032 Red Arrow Hwy, Sawyer 49125; (269) 426-4013
www.michigandnr.com/parksandtrails/details.aspx?id=504&type=SPRK

This park features 3 miles of beaches that are wonderful places to play, run in the sand, or simply sunbathe. But it is the dunes themselves that will eventually draw you here. These are so large that they have been given names (not unlike mountain peaks), and some of the dunes are popular for sandboarding. If you need an escape from sun and surf, consider walking along a shaded hiking trail or exploring the flora of the dunes. This is one of the most popular beaches in Michigan, so be prepared for a crowd in some places. There are picnicking and camping facilities here, too.

15 Wilderness State Park

903 Wilderness Park Dr, Carp Lake 49718; (231) 436-5381
www.michigandnr.com/parksandtrails/details.aspx?id=509&type=SPRK

The beaches at Wilderness State Park are on the upper northwest shoulder of the L.P., in a wild and remote area. These are not the soft sand beaches of the south. The shoreline consists of a mix of conifers and hardwoods, and there are rocks and driftwood present; if you're looking for solitude, come here. There are even rustic cabins, so you can make this a northwoods getaway. The park is also quite large—10,000 acres—with inland lakes and trails to explore when you're not enjoying the waves and beaches. All told, this might be the best wilderness experience on the Lake Michigan shore.

Beaches & Dunes

16 Wm. C. Sterling State Park

2800 State Park Rd, Monroe 48162
www.michigandnr.com/parksandtrails/Details.aspx?id=497&type=SPRK

Amid all of the Great Lakes and their extremely long shorelines, it's often easy to forget Lake Erie, but that'd be a mistake. Located in the southeast portion of the state, Wm. C. Sterling State Park is easy to access, and with a mile-long beach, boat launches, fishing lagoons, campsites, and picnic areas, there's a lot to do. The wildlife viewing trails are an especially good diversion and the new River Raisin National Battlefield Park can be reached by a hiking trail from the park.

Beaches & Dunes

Mushroom Houses of Charlevoix

The history of a civilization is reflected, in part, in the buildings it creates. From mushroom houses to Calumet Theatre, the architecture of Michigan is as diverse as its landscape and history. Exploring these locations is a great way to learn about the state's history.

HISTORIC BUILDINGS & ARCHITECTURE

1 Calumet Theatre

340 Sixth St, PO Box 167, Calumet 49913; (906) 337-2610
www.calumettheatre.com/

The Calumet Theatre is a National Historic Landmark and represents the age of the copper boom, when the town was flourishing and could afford world-class entertainers. Today the theater is still going strong and hosts numerous shows for the public. Elaborately designed, the building is a 2-story Renaissance Revival structure, and the stone exterior is the gorgeous and multicolored Jacobsville sandstone. Highlights also include a copper roof and a clock and bell tower. The exterior of the theater represents the efforts of local architect Charles K. Shand. The elaborate interior was created by Chicago designer William Eckert.

2 Detroit Historic Districts

Cityscape Detroit, PO Box 43735, Detroit 48243; (313) 438-0295
www.cityscapedetroit.org/historic_districts.php

The city of Detroit has done something that every city needs to do: it has recognized its distinct neighborhoods and celebrated each area's specific history, architecture, the ethnicity of its residents and all that has helped contribute to making it unique and memorable. In each district, the historic buildings are described as is the architectural design. Each place is worthy of exploring by car, foot, bike or public transport. Detroit's neighborhoods are a reminder that cities are an agglomeration of developments, and often cities actually grow by absorbing other existing communities. You can't see all of the districts in one day, but they are worthy of many day trips with stops at local bars, restaurants and public places.

3 Fox Theatre

2211 Woodward Ave, Detroit 48201; (313) 471-3200
www.olympiaentertainment.com/default.asp?olympia=30&objId=1

Part of the Woodward historic area, this theater is still a vital part of the entertainment scene, but the building is so impressive we think it would be impossible to miss. The architecture is Siamese-Byzantine, a conglomeration of Far Eastern, Egyptian, Babylonian and Indian themes from various eras. This theater is on the National Register of Historic Places and on the list of National Historic Landmarks. The flagship of all Fox Theatres, it was built in 1928 and was the first to include speakers for sound films. As amazing as that all may seem, we are equally impressed by the fact that it has 5,048 seats. Always a trendsetter, it was visited by Shirley Temple at one stage and equipped for CinemaScope at another. And for you Elvis Presley fans, the King performed here in 1956. If you visit, try to watch the acts, as well as marvel at the architecture.

4 Heritage Hill—A National, State and Local Historic District

Heritage Hill Association, 126 College SE, Grand Rapids 49503; (616) 459-8950
www.heritagehillweb.org/

This neighborhood of 1,300 homes and businesses is Michigan's largest and finest collection of nineteenth- and twentieth-century American architecture. Dating back to 1843, this neighborhood was slated for demolition due to a variety of urban renewal developments in the 1960s. Neighbors worked diligently to place Heritage Hill on the National Register of Historic Places. This designation in 1971 effectively stopped the demolition of more than 75 percent of the neighborhood. It is a wonderful example of how residents with pride can rescue their community and preserve the past for today and for the future. Self-guided walking tour information is available at the website. An annual Weekend Tour of Homes is held the third weekend in May.

5 Hoyt Public Library

Public Libraries of Saginaw, Hoyt Public Library, 505 Janes Ave, Saginaw 48607; (989) 755-0904
www.saginawlibrary.org/

This is one of the most impressive buildings we saw in Michigan. A gift of lumber baron Jesse Hoyt to the City of Saginaw, this elaborate design was created by the architectural firm of Van Brunt and Howe of Boston after a nationwide competition was held. An eye-catching building, the library features limestone blocks from a Bay Port quarry and a trim of red sandstone, from Lake Superior quarries, that makes for a high contrast. With work beginning in 1887, we have to admire how they created the complex lines and used the heavy material. The Hoyt Public Library opened in 1890 and continues to be a fascinating structure both inside and out.

6 | Lakeshore Museum Center

430 W Clay Ave, Muskegon 49440-1002; (231) 722-0278
The Hackley and Hume Historic Site, 484 W Webster Ave, Muskegon 49440-1046
http://lakeshoremuseum.org/

The museum has permanent and changing exhibits that explore the natural and cultural history of the area. Exhibits include a 400-million-year journey through Michigan in the making, animal habitats, and a life-sized mastodon. Two hands-on galleries are designed for younger museum visitors. The Hackley and Hume homes are some of the finest examples of Queen Anne style Victorian homes in the country. Designed by David S. Hopkins of Grand Rapids and built in the late 1880s, they feature lavish woodcarvings, stenciling, stained glass windows, and period furnishings. The Scolnik House of the Depression Era, with period furnishings and appliances, tells the story of a couple of families living during the Great Depression. The history of firefighting is told next door at the Fire Barn Museum. Exhibits include hose carts, hook and ladder trucks, uniforms, and photographs of some of the area's most devastating fires.

7 | Meadow Brook Hall

480 S Adams Rd, Rochester 48309; (248) 364-6263, (248) 364-6200
www.meadowbrookhall.org/

A classic example of Tudor style architecture, this was the home of Matilda Dodge Wilson, heiress to the fortune of the Dodge Motor Car Company. Built just before the Great Depression, the house includes a famous collection of art objects. Another claim to fame for the house is the fact that its 88,000 square feet and 110 rooms make it one of the largest homes in the Midwest.

8 | Michigan State Capitol

State Capitol Building, 100 Capitol Ave, Lansing 48933; (517) 373-2353
www.michigan.gov/miplaces

We are constantly fascinated by the ideas and concepts that are incorporated into the architecture of state capitols, which are, after all, the centers of state power. Michigan's present capitol building is her third. (The first was in Detroit, the second in Lansing.) Designed by Elijah E. Myers, the Renaissance Revival building took 6 years to construct, opening on January 1, 1879. The building contains 9 acres of hand-painted Victorian decorative paint, and includes many interesting faux finishes, including pine painted to mimic walnut and cast iron that mimics marble. The building still contains many of its original elements, including the black and white Vermont limestone and marble floors, as well as an interesting glass floor composed of 976 tiles in the capitol's rotunda. A beautiful cast iron and tin dome soars above, decorated with stars and muses that show the way to Michigan's future, inspiring citizens and visitors alike!

9 Mushroom Houses of Charlevoix

Charlevoix Visitor Bureau, 109 Mason St, Charlevoix 49720; (800) 367-8557, (231) 547-2101
www.oldhousejournal.com/mushroom-houses-of-charlevoix/magazine/1666
www.visitcharlevoixmichigan.com/stories/earl_young_architect_builder_mush-room_houses_charlevoix_michigan

How can we describe Earl Young's Unique Mushroom Houses? All the adjectives must have been used already: weird, quirky, whimsical, hobbit houses, gnome homes, fairy tale homes, imagination dwell-ings, unforgettable houses! You have to take a walk in the Charlevoix neighborhood where this world-famous group of homes can be found. The residents bought these fascinating, one-of-a-kind homes, so they must be used to lots of gawkers; however, these are private homes, so please honor their privacy. From 1918 to 1950, Young designed 30 stone homes, and each one is a unique work of art. With stone walls capped by mushroom-like cedar roofs, windows outlined by boulders, and chimneys and doorways framed by large stones, these are sights to behold. The best way to experience these houses is to simply take a walk on the sidewalk; just remember that while a map and descriptions are readily available, these are still private residences.

10 Osceola Quilt Trail

PO Box 301, Tustin 49688
www.osceolaquilttrail.org/

Following the lead of quilt trails in other states, the Osceola Quilt Trail is the result of a creative effort by businesses, residents and barn own-ers to decorate buildings with quilt designs. It is not the architecture here that is important, but rather the quilting designs and patterns. This trail is a fun way to explore the rural landscape and forms a type of scavenger hunt. From quilt-bedecked barns to post offices, the quilt trail connects rural roads with Marion, Tustin, LeRoy, Hersey, Evart and Reed City. When we visited the area, there were 77 designs and the number is sure to continue to grow.

11 Superior Dome

1401 Presque Isle Ave, Marquette 49855-5301; (906) 227-1000
www.nmu.edu/sportsathletics/node/229

This may not be the most beautiful architectural site in the state, but it is certainly one that is unique. In 2010, the Superior Dome, the sports stadium of Northern Michigan University–Marquette, set a world record. It was honored as the world's largest dome (by diameter) and the largest wooden dome structure. To let you know how big it is, there are 781 Douglas fir beams supporting this massive roof. In a place that has tremendous amounts of lake-effect snow, this geodesic dome supports up to 60 pounds per square foot and provides a safe environment for the Northern Michigan Wildcats football team. The stadium is also versatile. Its artificial surface can be winched in and out on a cushion of air; in this way, the surface can be used for football, soccer and field hockey and then replaced for basketball, volleyball and ice hockey.

12 William G. Thompson House Museum and Gardens

101 Summit St, Hudson 49247; (517) 448-8125
http://thompsonmuseum.org/

This Queen Anne style home was built in 1890 and is listed on the National Register of Historic Places. It includes an ornate metal roof and a cut stone foundation. The interior features Eastern art from William Thompson's personal collection. The gardens are an integral part of a visit; the gardens include a privet hedge surrounding a formal garden. A large copper beech tree is a landmark for the location, and the roses are a delight of summer color.

Henry Ford Museum

If you were to list the 50 states in a word association game, Michigan would be too easy. Yes, it is the peninsula state, and yes, it is the Great Lakes state, but most of all it is the automotive state. When we think of Detroit, it's not the Tigers, Red Wings, Pistons and Lions that come to mind first, it is the automobiles—Ford, Chrysler and General Motors. Michigan is the epicenter of everything automotive, and there are opportunities to explore automotive history throughout the state.

CARS & TRUCKS

1 Automotive Hall of Fame

21400 Oakwood Blvd., Dearborn 48124; (313) 240-4000
www.automotivehalloffame.org/

What makes an Automotive Hall of Fame? We know that the automobile has become more than an American icon; it is an essential part of both our economy and social world. And the automobile is the basis for this museum about automotive pioneers and innovators. The world of the automobile is immortalized in the Hall of Honor, which includes an 11x65-foot mural and 90 individual images. Here important stories that are often lost to the current generation can be found, such as the tale of Alice Ramsey, the first woman to drive across the country, and background about Zora Arkus-Duntov, who is forever linked to the Corvette. The displays and exhibits, as well as the individuals that are honored, present a fascinating history of the car.

2 Brockway Mountain Drive

www.dnr.state.mi.us/publications/pdfs/wildlife/viewingguide/up/13Keweenaw/index.htm

Located on the northern tip of Keweenaw Peninsula, Brockway Mountain Drive is a wonderful drive noted for its scenery and lovely setting. Only 9.5 miles long, this uphill drive offers some of the most stunning views of Lake Superior and the harbor at Copper Harbor. This is also the highest drive above sea level between the Rockies and the Alleghenies. To add to its appeal, this is also an official Michigan Wildlife Viewing Area. Truth be told, the entire drive up the peninsula qualifies as a scenic highway for us, but Brockway is the frosting on the cake. On a clear day you might see Isle Royale and on any given day you might be able to spot one of the big "salties"—ocean-going cargo vessels.

3 Byways to Flyways

www.mac-web.org/Projects/DiscoverOurWildSide/BywaysToFlyways.htm

Combining a driving tour and a bird watching trip is a great idea. Centering a bird watching trip on the diverse habitats of the Detroit River and western Lake Erie ensures both a variety of scenery and an abundance of species to spot. Two of the four great flyways of the continent converge here, and up to 350 species have been recorded. There are 27 birding sites along this route and eight Important Bird Areas. Besides the area's many songbirds, waterfowl and shorebirds are common here. The edge of the forest is a route for raptors that prefer to avoid flying over open water.

4 Ford Museum

The Henry Ford, 20900 Oakwood Blvd., Dearborn 48124-5029; (313) 982-6001, (800) 835-5237
www.hfmgv.org/

This museum is so large that you need to take breaks for food, maybe even a film or a visit to the Rouge Factory or Greenfield Village. Then it's time to return and see more. They rightfully boast of housing 26 million artifacts, and we can guarantee you will not come close to seeing all of these or even all the individual exhibits. This is history as told through the windshield of our automobiles. Many of the exhibits, such as the Oscar Mayer Wienermobile, are lighthearted. Others, such as the limo that JFK rode in when he was shot and the bus where Rosa Parks made her courageous stand, are emotional. Make sure you give yourself plenty of time when you visit.

5 Ford Rouge Factory

The Henry Ford, 20900 Oakwood Blvd., Dearborn 48124-5029; (800) 835-5237
www.thehenryford.org/rouge/index.aspx

We saw this factory decades ago, and it is fascinating to return and see all the changes. Now there is a tour and presentation to match its modern assembly process. There are two theaters, an observation deck and a gallery that offer information, background and a little dramatics to your visit. There were originally 93 active buildings in this complex. With ore docks, steel furnaces, rolling mills, glass furnaces, and even their own power plant, Ford controlled the entire process from raw materials to finished products. The railroads and shipyards were as impressive as the final assembly area. At one time more than 100,000 people worked at the plant. We also liked the fact that the Rouge Living Laboratory has revitalized the brownfield setting. Wetlands and green roofs are a measure of their success.

Cars & Trucks

6 Gilmore Car Museum

6865 Hickory Rd, Hickory Corners 49060; (269) 671-5089
www.GilmoreCarMuseum.org/

Entering the main exhibit hall and the 90-acre historic campus is breathtaking. We were overwhelmed by both the number of vehicles and their superb condition. The Automobile Heritage Center has more than 300 cars. We were hard-pressed to find a favorite, but in the end it was a toss-up between the Dueseneberg and the Tucker. There is also a 1930s service station, vintage pedal cars, and the Blue Moon Silk City 1941 Diner. A motorcycle collection and even nostalgia pieces (such as the collection of hood ornaments) are additional treats. In the summer, numerous events and car shows make this museum an experience for a full day or even a weekend.

7 Highway 41 Historic Road Trip

www.state-ends.com/michigan/us41/

US 41 is a fascinating option for drivers. A U.S. highway that runs north-to-south, it begins at a cul-de-sac near Fort Wilkins and Copper Harbor (as close to Lake Superior as you can get) and the highway does not stop until it gets to Miami, Florida.

The route crosses the U.P. and enters Wisconsin, where it crosses over the Menominee River between Menominee, and Marinette, Wisconsin. The towns along the route from Copper Harbor to Menominee include Escanaba, Rapid River, Marquette, L'Anse, Houghton and Hancock.

8 Michigan International Speedway

12626 US 12, Brooklyn 49230-9068; (800) 354-1010
www.mispeedway.com/

Home to one of the largest single-day sporting events in the state, this is Michigan's home for automobile racing. With wide curves, it is known as the fastest track in NASCAR. For those interested in packing in a weekend of fun around the various races, camping is available, as are package deals.

9 Model T Automotive Heritage Complex

Model T Automotive Heritage Complex Inc, 461 Piquette Ave, Detroit 48202
www.tplex.org

Is there a car that is more famous or more iconic than the Model T? It was not the first car, but it was the first mass-produced car with replaceable parts. This is where the age of the automobile began; this plant eventually became the world's largest automobile factory and the beginning of the "Motor City." Today, it is a museum of early automobiles and includes Studebakers, Hupmobiles and many other now-obscure brands. You can also see Henry Ford's office here. One warning as you plan, the facility has limited hours and you have to check in ahead of time.

10 Motorsports Museum

Motorsports Hall of Fame of America, PO Box 194, Novi 48376-0194;
(248) 349-RACE, (248) 349-7223
www.mshf.com/museum/

If there is a motorized contest involved, it's probably recognized here. Whether they involve stock cars, powerboats, airplanes or snowmobiles, there are many different kinds of motorized races. The museum's videos and exhibits—not to mention the race machines on display—help you learn about them all. This is a place for motorheads, a spot that honors the great racing personalities and gathers the racing fans and wannabes. When I visited, I really liked the Ford 999 racer from 1902 because it reminded me of the vehicle my grandfather was driving when he was courting my grandmother. You will probably find some stories and vehicles that will bring back memories for you, too.

11 Pierce Stocking Scenic Drive

Sleeping Bear Dunes National Lakeshore, 9922 Front St, Empire 49630;
(231) 326-5134
www.nps.gov/slbe/planyourvisit/psscenicdrive.htm

Located within Sleeping Bear Dunes National Lakeshore, this drive is located between Empire and Glen Arbor and connects scenic vistas you can explore on short walks. Large sand dunes, forests, inland lakes, and Lake Michigan's shores are among the highlights for bikers and drivers. There are markers along the route that match the book provided by the national park with insights about the scenery. This scenic drive was named for Pierce Stocking, a lumberman who created the road in the 1960s to share his love of the area's beauty. Little and Big Glen Lakes, Lake Michigan's Manitou Islands and Lake Michigan's Sleeping Bear Bay are wonderful scenic views. Many rate Lake Michigan's Overlooks 9 and 10 as the top attractions.

Cars & Trucks

12 R. E. Olds Transportation Museum

240 Museum Dr., Lansing 48933; (517) 372-0529
http://reoldsmuseum.org/

This is the birthplace of the Oldsmobile. Driving around Michigan, we were fascinated to learn about the origins of the individual car brands that were eventually absorbed into one of the large manufacturers. Visiting this site we learned that Lansing is about more than just cars; it also has a long history in powered lawn mowers. R. E. Olds designed the original "Lansing-made" mower in 1916. Of course, there's a clear connection to the automobile industry here, with the history of the Olds Motor Works, the REO Motor Car Company, and the story of Ransom Eli Olds himself. Engines, automobiles and other memorabilia make this a stop to remember.

13 River Road National Scenic Byway

http://byways.org/explore/byways/10781

This drive through Huron National Forest Drive winds past forests and along streams to Oscoda, near Lake Huron. Along the way, views of the Au Sable River will tempt you to put in a canoe, and that's just one of the recreational opportunities along the route. There's also hiking, cross-country skiing, fishing, hunting and bird watching. In Oscoda, visit the Lumberman's Monument, and a visitor's center, which will connect you with the lumber industry's past. An interpretive site at Largo Springs will take you, via boardwalk, to a spectacular view of the Largo Springs and the river below.

14 Road to Hell

www.upnorthmichigan.com/Drives/roadtohell.htm

Perhaps we should have a warning here—BEWARE: HELL AHEAD. Probably not, but it is a fun idea and the road to Hell (Michigan) actually does exist. The ride will take you over hills, along beautiful lakes and rivers, and through an archway of trees. Long popular for motorcycles, this is a good route for cars, too. D-32 goes from Gregory to Hell, but you will have to look to find it. The highlights of the road include Edwin George Reserve, Gosling Lake, Half Moon

Lake and Brum Lake. The road can be a little rough, but is well worth it. Horseback riding, kayaking, fishing and picnicking can add to your fun. As for Hell, we can tell you it is not too big and if it means anything in context of its name—it is near a dam! The founder was George Reeves, who started with lumber mills and ended up with a whiskey mill on Hell Creek. This town does offer some unique namesakes like a "fully non-accredited" diploma, Screams Ice Cream, and Hell in a Handbasket.

15 Tunnel of Trees

Cross Village
www.upnorthmichigan.com/Drives/tunneltrees.htm

This was one of our favorite drives in Michigan. It follows Highway 119 from Harbor Springs to Cross Village through a dense stand of forest. With the sunlight filtering through the canopy and glimpses of Lake Michigan, there is plenty to see and enjoy in the summer, but the colors in autumn are amazing. Be prepared to go slowly so you can fully enjoy the ride. Give yourself a break and an opportunity to see the landscape by stopping at the Thorne Swift Nature Preserve halfway along the drive.

16 Walter P. Chrysler Museum

One Chrysler Dr, I CIMS 488-00-00, Auburn Hills 48326-2778; (888) 456-1924
http://wpchryslermuseum.org/

I will never forget my grandmother's 1957 Chrysler and my father's old Desoto. For me, these were the symbols of the Chrysler Corporation, but many of you will likely think of other vehicles, too. Chrysler was founded by Walter P. Chrysler, a machinist and a railroad mechanic from Kansas who was recruited by General Motors and began his own automotive empire. We sometimes forget the modest beginnings of our automotive giants, and with its exhibits, cars and interactive displays, this museum captures part of that journey. From technologically impressive displays to the lower floor, which feels more like a garage, this is living history. Be sure to visit the Boss Chrysler Garage, which is home to everything from muscle cars to prototypes.

17 Whitefish Bay National Forest Scenic Byway

http://byways.org/stories/58469

Whitefish Bay National Forest Scenic Byway is in Hiawatha National Forest in the U.P. of Michigan. This route is parallel to the North Country National Scenic Trail and is a good place to combine walking and driving, which we found to be an inspiring way to enjoy the scenery. The hiking trail is in good shape here and Lake Superior is nearby and a vivid blue. Be sure to follow the route out to Naomikong Creek, and stop by to observe the gorgeous shallow waters of Tahquamenon Bay. Its sandy beaches and the warm waters are an inviting place to experience the big lake. At the far end of the bay, you can explore Point Iroquois Lighthouse and beach.

18 Woodward Avenue Dream Cruise

www.woodwarddreamcruise.com/About/History.aspx
http://byways.org/explore/byways/13754/

The Motor City is the perfect place for the Dream Cruise: originally a soccer fund-raiser, this event has become one of the premier car cruises in the world. Today, more than 250,000 participants and 1.5 million spectators enjoy seeing 40,000 classic cars drive down Woodward Avenue, America's first highway. This ride is now referred to as "Drivin' from Drive-In to Drive-In" and includes visiting the classic restaurants that dot the route. The historic drive-ins like Ted's and the Totem Pole are reason enough to journey to this event. So get in the car, turn on the rock and roll, roll down the bobby socks, and cruise.

Cars & Trucks

19 Ypsilanti Automotive Heritage Museum & Miller Motors Hudson

100 E Cross St, Ypsilanti 48198; (734) 482-5200
http://ypsiautoheritage.org/

We really enjoyed this site. Not only is there a wonderful collection of cars from several now-extinct car brands, such as Hudson and Kaiser-Frazer, but this was and still is Miller Motors Hudson, a car dealership that has never gone out of business. Car shows are held here, and you will enjoy visiting with the museum caretaker/Hudson dealer who has more stories and information than you can possibly take in, but it is so fun to engage in conversation as you wander through the rooms. You will also see cars in the process of being restored in the repair shop. Some highlights include the 1933 Hudson Terraplane K Series Coach and a 1952 Hudson Hornet NASCAR champion driven by Herb Thomas—his story provided the inspiration for the 2006 Pixar film *Cars*. Old-timers like me will enjoy the advertising and promotional materials as well. Two blocks away from the museum there is a magnificent firefighter's museum, so you can plan a really full day.

Cars & Trucks

Grand Hotel Mackinac Island

Only you can determine what makes for a romantic or fun getaway, as the terms can be so subjective. Sometimes it's just a quiet place to watch the sunset or a view of a bay filled with sailboats, or it could be a raucous party at a pool. For those of us who are seniors, our sense of what's romantic and fun differs—so in this section we are looking at a sense of place that contrasts strongly with our busy daily lives.

FUN GETAWAYS

1 Castle in the Country Bed and Breakfast Inn

340 M-40 South, Allegan 49010; (269) 673-8054
www.castleinthecountry.com/

This refurbished Victorian mansion is now "The Castle" and offers themed rooms for your getaway. With suites, whirlpools and fireplaces, this 10-room inn provides all the amenities, including kayaks and paddleboats that visitors can use on the private lake. The wooded trails wind through the forest and are great places to exercise and reflect. Side-by-side massages are a nice option for couples, and the spa offers a complete list other services.

2 Chateau Chantal

15900 Rue de Vin, Traverse City 49686; (800) 969-4009, (231) 223-4110
www.chateauchantal.com/

In an attempt to offer the ideal experience, the Chateau has created many packages visitors can choose from. A wine-pairing and dinner package is just one of the special options you can consider. Situated on a peninsula, the Chateau sits amid a sea of fruit trees and vines and is removed from the noise and energy of Traverse City, providing a quiet place to get away. When coupled with the gleaming water of Grand Traverse Bay, the 65 acres surrounding the Chateau are perfect for photography, painting or simple relaxation. If you're staying at the inn, the tasting room is close to the guest rooms and there is a variety of wine to choose from. Cooking classes are offered from January through April; details are available at the website.

3 Chicago Pike Inn & Spa

215 E Chicago St, Coldwater 49036; (517) 279-8744
www.chicagopikeinn.com/

Midway between the Great Lakes, this retreat is easy to get to from South Bend, Chicago or Detroit. The inn is more than 110 years old, but you will still find modern conveniences within this historic setting. With Coldwater Lake and another 100 lakes nearby to choose from, this is a retreat where fishing, boating, and opportunities for other outdoor activities surround you. Another option is nearby Allen, which has dubbed itself the "Antique Capital of the World." Golfing is another recreational option. And then there is always the option to just relax.

4 Crystal Mountain

12500 Crystal Mountain Dr, Thompsonville 49683-9742; (231) 378-2000
www.crystalmountain.com/

A destination for the entire family, this resort is a great place to be any time of the year. In summer, it offers 36 holes of golf, indoor and outdoor pools, tennis courts, mountain biking, and Michigan's only Alpine Slide. In winter, it features downhill and cross-country skiing, ice skating and snowshoeing. Visitors can enjoy some amenities year-round, such as the fitness center, a variety of dining options, and the Crystal Spa, which emphasizes renewal and relaxation with a variety of spa services. Even better, the resort is LEED-certified as environmentally friendly, honoring the beauty of northern Michigan in a mountain oasis.

5 Frankenmuth Bavarian Inn Lodge

Covered Bridge Ln, Frankenmuth 48734; (989) 652-7200
http://bavarianinn.com/

This is as German as you are going to get in Michigan—think of it as an international trip without a passport. The shops, the restaurants and the architecture are designed to transport you to another place, and your only obligation is to relax. When you're here, grab some spaetzle and wash it down with a local beer. Then, walk the waterfront and check out the wooden bridge and glockenspiel. This is also a town of festivals, so take a look at the list of 40 options and schedule your visit to participate in the merriment.

6 Garden Grove Bed & Breakfast

9549 Union Pier Rd, Union Pier 49129; (800) 613-2872
www.gardengrove.net/

Located in Harbor County and close to Warren Dunes State Park, this is a wonderful option for experiencing cottage living. Close to Chicago, but far enough away to be a true escape, this bed and breakfast is a popular destination for weddings and anniversaries. Nearby communities offer beaches, restaurants, golf courses and shopping, while the rooms will encourage you to lounge and relax. A casino and local wine trail offer more options. This Green Lodging Michigan partner provides elegance and grace while minimizing its environmental impact.

Fun
Getaways

75

7 Grand Hotel

286 Grand Ave, PO Box 286, Mackinac Island 49757; 800-33-GRAND, 800-334-7263
www.grandhotel.com/

Is it the island setting, the lack of cars, the historic furnishings, the grandeur of the building, or the world-famous surroundings that make this 1887 building so popular and in demand? *Travel + Leisure* magazine lists it as one of the top 500 hotels in the world. Every visit here is different, as each room is slightly different. Whichever room you stay in, the rocking chairs on the "world's largest porch" beckon and are one of the most inviting places for reading and relaxation in Michigan. One warning before you go: there are modern conveniences, but nothing about the overall hotel is modern except price, of course.

8 The Heather House Bed & Breakfast

409 N Main St, Marine City 48039; (810) 765-3175
www.theheatherhouse.com/

This 1888 Queen Anne Victorian house overlooks the St. Clair River, which is part of the Great Lakes and St. Lawrence Seaway. At one time Marine City was the biggest shipbuilding community on the Great Lakes, and many ship captains resided here. Now it is a place of natural beauty called Blue Water. This means that as you sit and relax at this beautiful bed and breakfast, you can watch upbound and downbound lake freighters pass by instead of traffic. With private bathrooms and outdoor porches, the bed and breakfast ensures you'll enjoy your stay in privacy and comfort.

9 The Historic Webster House

900 5th St, Bay City 48708; (989) 316-2552, (877) 229-9704
www.historicwebsterhouse.com/

This Queen Anne Victorian house has received the honor of being added to the Select Registry of Distinguished Inns of North America, a directory of unique travel destinations. Surrounded by Bay City's historic district and just a few blocks from the waterfront, the interior of this 1886 house has been renovated to meet the highest standards of elegance and style. Popular for weddings and other events, this bed and breakfast is a getaway for honeymooners and romantic travelers of all ages. It features European-style feathertop queen-sized beds and down duvets to snuggle into. A formal dining room creates the ideal setting for breakfasts and other special meals.

10 The Homestead

1 Wood Ridge Rd, Glen Arbor 49636; (231) 334-5000
www.thehomesteadresort.com/

Many of Michigan's retreats are literally award-winning, and this is no exception: it was voted the "Most Beautiful Place in America" by viewers of ABC's *Good Morning America*. How do we add to that? With a spa that sits on a ridge overlooking Lake Michigan and the pristine landscape of the Sleeping Bear Bay and Manitou Islands. A setting fit for reflection, tranquility and meditation in surrounding terraces, gardens and labyrinth. If you seek other escapes, swimming, biking, hiking, sailing and other options are available. Lodging options at The Homestead include The Inn, Stony Brook Lodge, Little Belle, and Fiddler's Pond, as well as privately owned condominiums and resort homes. When it comes to dining at the resort, like everything else at The Homestead, it's meant to make your vacation memorable. That means fresh ingredients, locally sourced when possible. It means stunning settings, with friendly, professional service. It means leaving the choice between fine dining and a simple salad to you.

11 The Inn at Bay Harbor

3600 Village Harbor Dr, Bay Harbor 49770-8577
www.innatbayharbor.com/

Travel + Leisure magazine named this luxury resort one of "The World's Best Hotels." Owned by Marriott, this resort features a large campus, and it's associated with a championship golf course and has a day spa. The real treat, however, is the resort's location on Lake Michigan, which gives this already-special resort a stunning backdrop.

12 Inn at Black Star Farms

10844 E Revold Rd, Suttons Bay 49682; (231) 944-1251
www.blackstarfarms.com/inn/

The setting is the most impressive feature here: this inn is surrounded by 160 acres of orchards and vineyards with their seasonally changing appearance. The facilities are superb, too. Each contemporary-styled room has its own private bath, and some rooms have fireplaces or spa tubs. The inn also features sundecks, a sauna, and a bar to help you relax. Both a winery tasting room and the Leelanau Cheese Co. are on-site. (When you visit, start with a bottle of the house wine.) There are many food options, too. If there are no special events planned, dinners are served on weekends. If you're looking for a lunch, head to the Hearth & Vine Café. With all the food and drink, consider taking to the trails to burn off some calories and enjoy the sunshine.

13 Keweenaw Mountain Lodge

14252 US 41, Copper Harbor 49918; (906) 289-4403
http://atthelodge.com/ STA

Expect a rustic atmosphere, as this is cabin-based lodging at the tip of the remote Keweenaw Peninsula. Enjoy the meals, the setting, and the old-style wooden architecture. On cool evenings (which can happen in any season) there are fireplaces to sit in front of and relax. It is not luxury that draws people here; it is the mountainous landscape, the big lake, the adventure, and the remoteness of the area (and just maybe a little golfing at the lodge's 9-hole course).

14 Kingsley House Bed and Breakfast

626 W Main St, Fennville 49408; (866) 561-6425
www.kingsleyhouse.com/

This inn is surrounded by beaches in every direction, small towns that accommodate tourists, and a variety of entertainment options. People are drawn by the lake, the sunsets, the antiques, and the total experience, but everyone wants their lodging to anchor their stay—a comfortable place to relax between events. With a spa service, a concierge, and the option of enjoying Jacuzzis and fireplaces, this bed and breakfast offers a perfect place to relax.

15 Lake 'N Pines Lodge

10354 Mud Lake Rd, Interlochen 49643; (231) 275-6671
www.lakenpineslodge.com/

This lodge is surrounded by Pere Marquette State Forest and is close to Traverse City. Located on Lake Dubonnet, this is a peaceful place and the lake offers good fishing. The forest is the perfect place to walk, bird watch or look for flowers. All of this peace and quiet is your home base and you can stay here or use it to explore the local communities, parks and wineries. With only the lodge and a few homes on the lake, you will feel as though you have discovered an unknown wilderness that is home to loons, ospreys and a variety of wildlife. This area is also the home of the Interlochen Center for the Arts (see The Fine Arts chapter), and catching a concert or performance can be the highlight of any vacation retreat.

16 Laurium Manor Inn

320 Tamarack St, Laurium 49913; (906) 337-2549
www.laurium.info/

A 1908 copper mine owner created this 45-room antebellum-style mansion that has become an inn with 18 guest rooms. A National Historic Site, most rooms have a private bath, whirlpool, fireplace and private balconies, which certainly meets our definition of a mansion. Just make sure your schedule allows time to explore the tiled porch, the library, the den and the parlor, as well as the rare hand-painted murals, antiques and furnishings. The breakfast each day is a full buffet. Across the street is a Victorian Hall that is run in conjunction with Laurium Manor Inn, and it offers more lodging options for travelers.

17 Portage Point Historic Inn & Lakefront Resort

8513 Portage Point Dr, Onekama 49675; (800) 878-7248
www.portagepointinn.com/

Since 1903, this inn and resort has been emphasizing family vacations. It is located on the inland Portage Lake but is only a short walk from Lake Michigan's sandy beach. With a new marina, this is a welcome location for boaters and fishing. They offer many activities for children, and adults can enjoy golf and a casino, among many other options.

Located on a wooded peninsula, the inn borders both lakes, and an inland channel provides protection and a haven when weather is challenging. Many experienced visitors recommend bringing food to grill, so you do not have to leave the comfort of the inn and beach. Consider visiting in winter for a cozy stay that involves some tobogganing and skiing.

18 Rosemont Bed and Breakfast

83 Lakeshore Dr, Douglas 49406; (269) 857-2637
www.rosemontinn.com/

Enjoy the warmth of a fireplace after a day of exploring the beach in summer or a day skiing the trails in winter. The local art galleries and the scenic views of Lake Michigan are both sources of inspiration, and biking and hiking offer quiet ways to explore the area. The bed and breakfast also has an outdoor pool, a coffee and tea bar, and a waterfall meditation garden. Even though there are many activities to occupy your time, we'd recommend setting aside some time for quiet contemplation. If that doesn't make you feel pampered enough, you can retire to your 4-poster bed for a night of quiet rest.

19 Stafford's Bay View Inn

2011 Woodland Ave, Petoskey 49770; (231) 347-2771
www.staffords.com/bayview

This inn, and especially its outside veranda, offer an excellent chance to enjoy the view of the lake. This 1886 inn harks back to the romance of historic times and maintains a lodge just a stone's throw from the mild waves of Little Traverse Bay. It is conveniently located near a bike trail and a wonderful waterfront park and only a short distance from downtown and all its tasty treats. The inn also offers the Roselawn Dining Room, which is a very popular dining destination.

20 The Vineyard Inn on Suttons Bay

1338 N Pebble Beach Dr, Suttons Bay 49682; (231) 941-7060
http://vininn.com/

Located in the wine country of Leelanau Peninsula, The Vineyard Inn promotes romantic escapes and offers 12 suites with views of their own private lawn and beach. The inn's rooms have a European flair; the beds are carved wood and feature pillow-top mattresses. Each room also comes with a wine bar and private balcony. Unlike most of the resorts that border Lake Michigan, this one faces east and offers an opportunity to wake up with an inspiring sunrise before going for a walk or ride, or bird watching. There are a variety of relaxing lawn games available, too, including bocce ball, croquet and badminton. For those looking for more speed and action, beach volleyball is available. End with a dip in the bay, and your day is full. The inn also offers a limousine service to shepherd visitors to the area wineries. If that's not your thing, you can always visit the dunes and lighthouses.

21 Walloon Lake Inn

4178 W St, Walloon Lake 49796; (231) 535-2999
www.walloonlakeinn.com/

These are Ernest Hemingway's old stomping grounds, and like Hemingway, you might want to enjoy the clear waters and fishing of Walloon Lake. You can do so at the Walloon Lake Inn, but the inn has more than the lake to compete with, as its own restaurant has earned a reputation and has attracted national attention. Originally known as the Fern Cottage, this inn is nearly 100 years old and continues to provide quiet country ambiance. The steamboats may not tie up at the dock anymore, but the sense of history is still here.

Fun
Getaways

Dow Gardens

From the southern border to the U.P., Michigan's climate and habitat vary a great deal. The lake effect produced by the Great Lakes affects Michigan's weather patterns and growing season, which are different than in other northern states. For example, each lake has a steady temperature and this helps hold back the frost, allowing wonderful garden displays to persist from May through October. If anything can brighten one's day, it is a garden, but if you want an experience a little more on the wild side, explore the history of Michigan's forests and enjoy the shade found in the state's parks and arboretums.

GARDENS, FLOWERS, ARBORETUMS & FORESTS

A teddy bear in the garden, Harry Potter's herbal lessons, and Alice in Wonderland!

1 4–H Children's Garden

1066 Bogue St, East Lansing 48824; (517) 355-5191 ext 1-349
http://4hgarden.cowplex.com/

Inside and out, there are garden options to enjoy in every season on the Michigan State University campus. The garden's name is intended to attract children and pique their interest, but it should not put off adults who will also get great joy. This up-to-date effort to interest children in the world of plants moves from Alice in Wonderland to Harry Potter. A winding path of bricks (think Dorothy in *The Wizard of Oz*) moves everyone through the child-sized conservancy, which will challenge them and engage them to learn.

2 Anna Scripps Whitcomb Conservatory

Belle Isle Park, Conservatory Way & Inselruhe Ave, Detroit; (313) 821-5428
10 a.m. til 5 p.m., Wednesday through Sunday except on Thanksgiving, Christmas and New Year's Day
www.detroitmi.gov/DepartmentsandAgencies/RecreationDepartment/Conservatory.aspx
Belle Isle Conservancy, 8109 E Jefferson, Detroit 48214; (313) 331-7760;
www.belleisleconservancy.org/

This building, which dates back to 1904, is a historic monument in itself. Yet it isn't just a building, its Victorian design still houses beautiful flora and invites visitors to its warm and humid interior. Palms soar to the glass domes, and flowers and fruits are all around in abundance. If the humidity gets to be too much, you can dart into the cactus wing for a little drying out. If you have only a limited time, concentrate on the orchids, the Conservatory's primary claim to fame. In the summer, be sure to stroll the outdoor gardens, too.

3 Cooley Gardens

213 W Main, Lansing; (517) 483-4277
www.cooleygardens.org/

Most arboretums or public gardens are found at the edge of cities or in the suburbs, but the Cooley Gardens are nearly in the center of Lansing, just south of the state capitol and the central business district. It is a beautiful little "pocket" garden situated on just 1 acre of land. This semiformal garden has a very romantic feeling to it.

Maybe it is the English cottage garden design, which seems right out of a romance novel. We had a little challenge finding this garden, but it was worth the effort.

4 Dow Gardens

1809 Eastman Ave, Midland; (989) 631-2677
www.dowgardens.org/

This garden and arboretum was once the personal playground of Herbert Dow of Dow Chemical, but now it is open to the public. The flowers are grouped in a very unobtrusive way, so that you feel like you are making discoveries as you walk through the parkland forest. There are places of seclusion, open grass areas, showy roses, and tulips and seasonal displays. A quiet stream meanders through the gardens and conveys a sense of peace and meditation, while inviting birds to be part of your observations. Metal sculptures enhance the landscape, and a children's garden and organic vegetable display provide other diversions.

5 Farm Center at Kensington Metropark

2240 W Buno Rd, Milford 48380; (810) 227-8910, (248) 684-8632;
www.metroparks.com/metroparks/activities/index.aspx?Name=Farm+Center

Bringing a sense of farming to an urban population is important as more people become distanced from their agricultural roots. This farm center is both a walk back in time and a walk into nature. From maple syrup in the spring to pumpkins in the fall, there is always something happening here and opportunities to participate in the farm center. The restored barn, the kids cottage and the farm animals will charm the young ones and please parents.

6 Fernwood Botanical Garden and Nature Preserve

13988 Range Line Rd, Niles 49120; (269) 695-6491
www.fernwoodbotanical.org/visit.html

Fernwood is situated on the St. Joseph River between Buchanan and Niles, in southwest Michigan. Fernwood comprises 105 acres of gardens and natural areas. Visitors may enjoy woodlands, a prairie, cultivated gardens, an arboretum, springs, ponds, and walking and hiking trails. Other features include a nature center, fern conservatory, art gallery, library, cafe, and garden and gift shops. The garden features an herb garden, rock garden, boxwood garden, fern and hosta collections, railway garden, children's nature adventure garden, English cottage border, Japanese garden, and more. Fernwood offers something to engage every visitor.

7 Frederik Meijer Gardens & Sculpture Park

1000 E Beltline Ave NE, Grand Rapids 49525; (888) 957-1580, (616) 957-1580
www.meijergardens.org/

One of the world's most significant botanic and sculpture experiences, Frederik Meijer Gardens & Sculpture Park serves more than 550,000 visitors annually. Meijer Gardens was recently ranked in the top 100 most-visited art museums worldwide by *Art Newspaper*, the leading publication in global art news. The 132-acre grounds feature Michigan's largest tropical conservatory, one of the largest children's gardens in the country, arid and Victorian gardens with bronze sculptures by Degas and Rodin, a carnivorous plant house, outdoor gardens, including waterfalls, streams and wetlands, and a 1,900-seat outdoor amphitheater featuring an eclectic mix of world-renowned musicians every summer. The internationally acclaimed Sculpture Park features a permanent collection, including works by Rodin, Moore, Bourgeois and Plensa, among others. Indoor galleries host changing sculpture exhibitions with recent exhibitions by Picasso, Degas, di Suvero, Borofsky, Calder and Dine.

8 Hartwick Pines State Park and Logging Museum

4216 Ranger Rd, Grayling 49738; (989) 348-7068
www.michigandnr.com/parksandtrails/Details.aspx?type=SPRK&id=453

This is a garden that nature planted—49 acres of history and ecology in homage to the white pine, and a shelter to many other old-growth trees. These white pines are 250–400 years old and deserve our respect. After your orientation at the Visitor Center, you can go to the Hartwick Pines Logging Museum where you can learn about the early days of logging (1840–1910). You might have some mixed emotions, but that is all right. Done right, logging serves us and the forest well.

9 Hidden Lake Gardens

6214 Monroe Rd (M-50), Tipton 49287; (517) 431-2060
http://hiddenlakegardens.msu.edu/

Located in Michigan's "Irish Hills," there is much to find at this 755-acre plant bonanza, which is owned and maintained by Michigan State. This garden displays plants from both the temperate zone and those from the tropics. The tropical plants, housed in a dome, include cocao, papaya, coffee and tapioca, while a visit to the cactus dome is an escape to a different environment altogether. Plan to stop at the visitor center for an orientation.

10 Holland Tulips

Holland Area Visitors Bureau, 78 E 8th St, Holland 49423; (800) 506-1299, (616) 394-0000
http://holland.org/locations/404-history-of-tulip-time
www.tuliptime.com/events
www.holland.org/

Six million tulips bloom each spring throughout Holland, Michigan, and it all started with a Woman's Literary Club meeting in 1927. There, Miss Lida Rogers, a biology teacher at Holland High School, suggested that Holland adopt the tulip as the city's official flower and celebrate this with a festival. The idea caught on, and in 1928 the city council purchased 100,000 tulip bulbs from the Netherlands to plant in city parks and other areas. In the spring of 1929, thousands of tulips bloomed and the long history of the annual Tulip Time festival started. This early-May festival has grown considerably since then, with 8 days of fun: parades, entertainment, Klompen (wooden shoe) dancing, fireworks, and lots of Dutch food, merchandise and demonstrations. Of course, the number one attraction is still the tulip itself—and there are literally millions to see in the city parks, downtown planters, Tulip Lanes, and the Dutch attractions. Veldheer's Tulip Farm alone plants more than 5 million tulips every year. And if you want to bring a little of Holland's signature flower home with you, tulip bulbs are available for purchase starting late August and throughout the fall.

11 Loda Lake Wildflower Sanctuary

4794 6 Mile Rd, White Cloud 49349; (231) 745-4631
www.fs.fed.us/wildflowers/regions/eastern/LodaLake/index.shtml

We often wonder why so much time and money is spent on importing plants, landscaping, and forcing nonnative species to survive in our climate, especially when our nation's wildflowers are already here and beautiful. If you don't believe this, you need to visit Loda Lake in the Huron-Manistee National Forests. Maintained in a unique partnership

between the U.S. Forest Service and the Michigan Garden Clubs, this former white pine forest was logged in the 1890s by the railroad. Unable to convert it to farmland, landowners were happy to sell it to the national forest during the Depression. Today, you can enjoy more than 400 species in their natural settings. Follow the paths, carry a field guide and a camera (and binoculars because the birds like this area, too), and explore the diversity that comes with a little elevation change or a different angle of light. Special prizes to be found here include pink lady's slipper, jack-in-the-pulpit, pitcher plant, Indian pipe, swamp milkweed, and wild bergamot. For history buffs, you can also follow the cultural trail, which documents the fascinating history of prior owners and the logging/post-logging era. Trail maps are on-site.

12 Matthaei Botanical Gardens and Nichols Arboretum

1800 N Dixboro Rd, Ann Arbor 48105; 734-647-7600
Nichols Arboretum, 1610 Washington Hts, Ann Arbor 48104; 734-647-7600
www.lsa.umich.edu/mbg/

Matthaei Botanical Gardens is located on Ann Arbor's east side, and Nichols Arboretum is on the University of Michigan Central Campus. Both properties are owned by the University of Michigan. Together, they offer more than 700 acres of gardens, research areas and natural preserves. At the botanical gardens you will find highlights that include: a large conservatory with tropical, temperate and arid houses; Herb Knot Garden, a classic geometrically designed planting; Gateway Garden, filled with seasonal New World annuals, spring bulbs and native perennials; a children's garden, perennial garden and bonsai exhibit; a native prairie, woodland wildflowers and more. That is a lot to choose from, but you can always get oriented at the visitor center, where they can tell you what's in bloom and where the trails lead. Nichols Arboretum features collections of native and exotic shrubs and trees throughout its 123 acres, the largest collection of heirloom peonies in North America, a wetland boardwalk, Magnolia Glen, and a prairie. Each June, the Arboretum hosts Shakespeare in the Arb, a theater production that moves through the Arb. The Huron River flows along one of the boundaries of this spacious, glacially sculpted landscape, so you can enjoy views of it, too.

13 W. J. Beal Botanical Garden

E Kalamazoo St & W Circle Dr, East Lansing 48824; (517) 355-9582
http://msustatewide.msu.edu/Programs/Details/386

The oldest university botanical garden in the United States, this garden has more than 5,000 species of plants. Designed to make self-guided hikes easy, the plants are organized thematically: there are groupings based on evolutionary links, economic links, by landscape, and by ecosystem. We were surprised to see some plants considered invasive in the collection, but these were included to help people recognize them to prevent their spread. The gardens have weeds and prized garden varieties, herbs and poisonous plants, fibers and dyes, medicines, and perfumes—and much more than that. For instance, in the garden themed by evolution, the plants are arranged according to the evolutionary timescale. In addition, the garden is home to a variety of plants that are threatened, endangered or rare in Michigan.

14 W. K. Kellogg Experimental Forest

7060 N 42nd St, Augusta 49012; (269) 731-4597
http://agbioresearch.msu.edu/kelloggforest/index.html

While Hartwick Pines State Park features old-growth trees, W. K. Kellogg Experimental Forest highlights reforestation of abandoned agricultural land. This is primarily a research site of Michigan State University, but it is open to the public and anyone who has an interest in trees in general and forest management will likely enjoy a visit. Since 1931, scientists and arborists have worked on tree breeding and genetics, planting techniques and plantation management. The public can visit to learn tips for managing their own land and gain glimpses of ongoing research. The forest also provides recreation, such as bow hunting, trout fishing, jogging, picnicking, biking, hiking, horseback riding and cross-country skiing. There are a couple ways to enjoy the area when you visit: you can drive the loop or walk the interpretive trails.

Gardens, Flowers, Arboretums & Forests

Detroit Beer Company

Michigan is the place for good times and good beverages. With 90-plus microbreweries in the state, we could only offer a sample of the options. Your challenge is to try them all! Or if you prefer, just find the places near you and have a good time.

GOOD SPIRITS & GOOD TIMES

1 Arbor Brewing Company—ABC Brewpub

Arbor Brewing Pub & Eatery, 114 E Washington St, Ann Arbor 48104;
(734) 213-1393
www.arborbrewing.com/

We enjoyed the food and the setting at this brew pub, which was
ranked the "Best Brew Pub in the Midwest" by *BrewPub Magazine*.
In the summer, you can enjoy your meal at tables placed on the
sidewalk out front, a perfect setting for a great brew.

2 Bastone Brewery

419 S Main St, Royal Oak; (248) 544-6250
http://bastone.net/br/bastone-brewery

Restored to its Art Deco origins, this brewery is famous for its
Belgian-style microbrew; its Belgian Tripel won a Gold Medal at the
Great American Beer Festival. The selection expands from there.
The beer is accompanied by a variety of foods made from scratch
with fresh ingredients, including thin-crust pizzas and seafoods.
Better yet, the Bastone Brewery is only one of four distinct dining
options here. There are also Vinotecca, Café Habana, and Commune
to choose from. Vinotecca is wine-centric, Café Habana is a Latin-
Cuban-fusion restaurant, and Commune is a Parisian-themed lounge.

3 Beer and Wine Trail

www.laketolake.com/michigan-beer-wine-trail.php

The Michigan Lake to Lake Bed and Breakfast Association has created
a unique way to combine quality lodging with equally memorable
wine tasting: the Beer and Wine Trail. The trail pairs Michigan's
breweries and wineries with nearby bed and breakfasts, providing
a great way to enjoy Michigan. According to the Association,
winemaking in Michigan dates back to 1679 when the voyageurs
fermented grapes for their own consumption. Eventually the first
commercial vineyards were established in the 1800s. With an
interruption by Prohibition, the wine industry continued to grow, and
today Michigan features 70-plus wine producers and more than
10,000 acres of vineyards. If beer is your preference, beer tours can
be arranged too, including packages to help you brew your own.

Good Spirits &
Good Times

5 Bell's Eccentric Café

355 E Kalamazoo Ave, Kalamazoo; (269) 382-2332
www.bellsbeer.com/eccentric-cafe/

Because its beer is distributed in other states, Bell's has established more of a reputation than most other microbrews. This following makes the Eccentric Café a great place for a beer lover's pilgrimage. Everyone knows that if a beer is good in a bottle, it is even better on tap. Like all the microbrews, a sampler is an excellent way to taste the range of styles. The restaurant is laid back, spacious, and serves food that matches the quality of the beer. There is also an outside courtyard where you can enjoy beer and sun. When you are done, visit their beer store on the corner of the building.

5 Blue Cow Restaurant and Brew Pub

119 N Michigan Ave, Big Rapids 49307; (231) 796-0100
www.bluecowcafe.com/

This is a fresh-from-the-farm restaurant and a microbrewery and wine bar. The food is locally sourced, and the menu varies with the season. They ask that you come with an appetite and a sense of humor, as laughter and smiles are valued on the farm. What they don't make, they buy locally, such as the Michigan beers. The cuts of meat here will not look like the factory-replicated cuts found in other restaurants. Come here for fresh pork, vegetables, and baked goods just out of the oven. Also, be sure to check out the unique bathrooms, which receive rave reviews.

6 The B.O.B.

20 Monroe Ave NW, Grand Rapids 49503; (616) 356-2000
www.thebob.com/

The B.O.B. gets its name because of its big old building, which encompasses 70,000 square feet. It serves its own popular brews, pizzas and other pub food. The building itself houses a variety of different events—everything from billiards to jazz and dance to comedy.

7 Detroit Beer Company

1529 Broadway, Detroit 48226; (313) 962-1529
www.detroitbeerco.com/

Located in downtown Detroit, the Detroit Beer Company is close enough to Comerica Park, Ford Field and the theater district to be included in a nice evening on the town. Located in the restored Hartz Building, the

restaurant is a perfect fit, and when you go inside and see the massive brew tanks, you'll know that you have a lot of flavors to sample. A tasty, well-prepared bar menu accompanies the beers.

8 The Earle

121 W Washington St, Ann Arbor 48104; (734) 994-0211
http://theearle.com/

Imagine French and Italian country cuisine served to the sound of jazz. There's great wine, too. For 21 years and counting, The Earle's wine list has been included in *Wine Spectator's* "Best of Award of Excellence" list, a compilation of restaurants with superb wine offerings. This is old-fashioned dining and relaxation—jazz trios on Fridays, Saturdays with a feeling of the Sixties, and piano and guitar during the week. With its stone walls and high ceilings, the acoustics are good, and music from the likes of Errol Garner, Dave Brubeck, Duke Ellington and Ramsey Lewis makes The Earle a wonderful place to eat or enjoy polite conversation.

9 Fitzgerald's Eagle River Inn

Eagle River Inn, 5033 Front St, Eagle River; (906) 337-0666
www.eagleriverinn.com/

This inn was recently entirely remodeled, making it one of the premium places to stay near the beachfront. But our first encounter with the inn was at the restaurant and bar. With a good selection of single malt scotch (which is hard to find in this semi-remote part of the state), we found the atmosphere relaxing and the owners friendly and easy to visit with. There is a full bar and a restaurant with windows facing Lake Superior. The menu is full and varied, with excellent preparation. With 55 permanent inhabitants, you can safely call Eagle River a quaint coastal town, but with an old lighthouse, a tall waterfall and an extensive beach, there's a lot to do here. If you time it right, you and your companions can be bathed in sunset as you eat.

10 Frankenmuth Brewery Company

425 S Main St, Frankenmuth; (989) 262-8300
www.frankenmuthbrewery.com/

This city of festivals is a tourist mecca and the place to go for German-style beers, and the Frankenmuth Brewery Company is home to some of the best beer in town. Known as *Das Good Bier!*, this is one of Michigan's oldest breweries. Their lagers and ales have won many awards, so come, taste, and take a tour of the brewery. Frankie's Root Beer is also made here. The patio and outdoor dining along the Cass River will make the experience even more enjoyable. Their beers are consistently highly regarded by *Beer Advocate*.

11 Good Neighbor Organic Vineyard and Brewery

9825 Engles Rd, Northport 49670; (231) 386-5636
http://goodneighbororganic.com/

Advertised as the region's first (and only) certified organic vineyard, orchard, winery and microbrewery, this farm has been certified organic since 2001. Here you can enjoy the flavor of organic food, learn what the term "organic" means and why it is important. Grapes are the primary crop, and they grow them without artificial pesticides, herbicides or fertilizers, to allow the grapes to get the true flavor of the sun and soil. For those who get headaches from the sulfites added to most wines, you will find these to be sulfite-free. The winery is also known for their own hard ciders.

12 Lily's Seafood Grill and Brewery

410 S Washington Ave, Royal Oak; (248) 591-5459
www.lilysseafood.com/index.html

The Great Lake State has lots of shoreline but no seashore, but that is not a problem for seafood lovers at Lily's. Inspired by their Scottish grandmother, Lily Strange, the founders of this restaurant have made this the perfect venue for conversation, relaxation and a right-at-home feeling. The seafood has been a menu staple since 1999, and hand-crafted beers are expected to add to the dining pleasure. The menu has items such as sesame ahi tuna, calypso crab cakes, and crab-stuffed pork chops, served on tables covered with navigational maps. Even the décor is filled with shrimp and fish, but don't worry if your companion doesn't eat fish; there are a few pork and chicken options. *Beer Advocate* gives them a score of 87.

13 The Livery

190 5th St, Benton Harbor 49022; (269) 925-8760
http://liverybrew.com/

Located in the art district of a quiet beach town, The Livery serves great beers and excellent foods (such as their well-known stuffed pepper soup) that keep bringing people back for more. Live and lively music adds a festive mood to the basement bar. If the music and sound level are not to your liking, the outdoor patio is a pleasant escape. *Beer Advocate* gave The Livery a rating of 94 (exceptional).

14 Michigan House Café and Brew Pub

300 6th St, Calumet; (906) 337-1910
www.michiganhousecafe.com/

Thanks to its history as a mining town, Calumet has a history of beer drinking, so it is only appropriate that the town now has its own brew pub for visitors today. Located downtown and only 2 blocks from ski and snowmobile trails, the pub is ready to refresh you. This is a full-service restaurant in addition to the vintage pub, and there is lodging on the second floor. The pub is home to Red Jacket Brewing Company, which follows the tradition of Bosch Brewing. Bosch produced beer from 1905 to the 1970s (with a break during Prohibition) and became the beer of the U.P. When you visit, you'll want to take in the century-old stained glass windows and bar mural. The pub's Oatmeal Stout gets lots of rave reviews, and on many Fridays there is live music.

15 Michigan Wine and Beer Festival

Michigan International Speedway, Brooklyn; (800) 354-1010
www.MiWineandBeerFest.com

If you love Michigan's wines, beers and food, then you will want to get to the racetrack for this annual event. An opportunity to taste and compare more than 100 wines, this is the place to find out what Michigan has to offer, which wineries you want to visit, and which varieties you love to drink. A 1-day admission includes a limited amount of tasting tickets for both beer and wine. Add to your pleasure with seminars that can increase your knowledge.

16 Rochester Mills Beer Co.

400 Water St, Rochester 48307; (248) 650-5080
www.beercos.com/

This brewery is located in the building of the historic Western Knitting Mill. Sometimes I think breweries have been created to preserve old buildings. In this case, the brewery has done an excellent job of saving hardwood floors, columns, beams, and exposed brick walls. With good food, a neat building and excellent beer, there is nothing lacking here, so visit and enjoy the pool tables and the outdoor patio. There is live music on weekends and even a martini lounge.

17 The Wine Loft

161 E Michigan Ave, Kalamazoo 49007; (269) 343-9227
www.millenniumrestaurants.com/loft/

The Wine Loft in Kalamazoo has been described as "ultra-sexy" in one review. A true wine bar, The Wine Loft aims to be cosmopolitan and atmospheric. From the cocktail server to the soft background music, this restaurant encourages mixing and meeting and is an ideal place to share an appetizer and bottle. Their staff harbors a unique gift for pairing the perfect wine with the individual's personality and palate, and they truly seem to be spot on. If wine is not your drink, The Wine Loft carries a wide selection of beer and spirits. Referred to as "urban chic," this is a place for coming together via Twitter and social media to make a personal connection.

Fort Mackinac

From colonial forts and sites from the War of 1812 to the advent of shipping on the Great Lakes and the rise of Motor City, Michigan has played a unique role in the events that shaped the nation. You can explore some of this legacy at these sites. If you visit all of them, give yourself a passing grade in Michigan history!

MICHIGAN HISTORY

1 Calumet

200 Fifth St, Ste 105, Merchant & Miners Bldg., Calumet 49913; (906) 337-6246
www.mainstreetcalumet.com/
www.nps.gov/kewe/historyculture/downtown-calumet.htm

Once known as Red Jacket (named after a Seneca chief), Calumet is a town that is both historic and current, a part of a national park and a vibrant community with much to offer, including food, art, shops, a museum dedicated to firefighters, and a historic theater. Calumet is also home to the visitor center for Keweenaw National Historical Park and museums and monuments honoring the town's copper-mining past. There is also a festival that celebrates Calumet's Finnish heritage; it makes an excellent date to visit in August. The most dramatic story of Calumet was the Strike of 1913 (and the subsequent Italian Hall massacre), which was eventually the basis for a Woody Guthrie song. The strike is an important story and a contrast to the historic beauty and the pleasure of the current town.

2 Charles H. Wright Museum of African American History

315 E Warren Ave, Detroit 48201; (313) 494-5800
http://thewright.org/

When Detroit obstetrician Charles Wright opened this museum, the largest museum dedicated to the history and the accomplishments of African Americans, he did so with this motto: "And Still We Rise: Our Journey Through African American History and Culture." This museum is both inspiring and challenging. It is home to a slave gallery and one of the most emotional museum walks you'll find anywhere. Then it rises to pride in the accomplishments as it celebrates the impact many great African Americans have had in science, education, religion and politics. To get the full impact of this experience, allow yourself time to watch and listen to the many videos that are incorporated into the exhibits. This is not a museum that can be explored quickly. Treat yourself to a study of a history that has gone untold for too long.

3 Colonial Michilimackinac

102 W Straits Ave, Mackinaw City 49701; (231) 436-4100
www.mackinacparks.com/colonial-michilimackinac/

Located on the Straits of Mackinac near the historic lighthouse museum and the impressive Mackinac Bridge, this reconstructed fort tells a tale of intrigue and adventure. Travel back to the 1770s and learn about muskets and life on the frontier when French voyageurs and American Indians shared the site with British soldiers. Today, the costumed actors make this a lively place, and kids love the palisade walls and the feeling of the old fort. You can climb up to the top of the walls and take in the scenery from all directions. There are also special events that can really enhance your visit, such as Fort Fright or the King's 8th Regiment Encampment. But if you can't make the events, don't worry—every day is filled with fun. There are historical baseball games, lacrosse matches, ongoing archaeological digs, dances, music and storytelling.

4 Crossroads Village

6140 Bray Rd, Flint 48505; (810) 736-7100
www.geneseecountyparks.org/pages/crossroads

Need a break from the rush of daily life? Go back to a time when things were a whole lot simpler. Welcome to Crossroads Village. It's an authentic Great Lakes town from the turn of the last century, with more than 34 historic structures and a thriving community to welcome you. Ride the Huckleberry Railroad, catch a show at the Colwell Opera House or learn a trade from one of our craftspeople. It's a place out of history where you can make a little history of your own. And it's just around the corner, at your Genesee County Parks.

5 Fayette Historic State Park

13700 13.25 Ln, Garden 49835; (906) 644-2603
www.michigandnr.com/parksandtrails/Details.aspx?id=417&type=SPRK

As much as we enjoyed the 1867 townsite, Big Bay de Noc was so stunning that it was hard to concentrate entirely on this wonderful living museum of a village. Its tall limestone cliffs, green trees and beautiful blue water make for a stunning contrast. The village was the site of a manufacturer of pig iron for 24 years. Now that story is told in the exhibits within the historic buildings, as well as at the visitor center. Guided and self-guided tours bring the village to life. Following the trails allows you to explore the beautiful setting. You will have a tough time reconciling the idyllic view and setting today with the smoky, dirty smelting operation that once operated here.

6 | Fort Mackinac

PO Box 370, Mackinac Island 49757; (906) 847-3328
www.mackinacparks.com/

Mackinac Island is home to a state park and a community that boasts the oldest building in Michigan. On an island that is historical in every sense of the word, it's hard to focus on one area, but Fort Mackinac is really the centerpiece of this place. Once you are inside the stone walls, you'll be awash in history. There are costumed interpreters, and special events that place you in the middle of the War of 1812. (If you're lucky, you may even hear a cannon blast.) If talk of war is not your thing, there is a Tea Room for civilized reflection and one of the island's best views of the harbor. How significant is this historic site? In 1875 it was declared the second national park in the United States; only Yellowstone preceded it. Today, Fort Mackinac is managed as a Michigan state park.

7 | Fort St. Joseph Archaeological Site

Fort St. Joseph Museum, 508 E Main St, Niles 49120; (269) 683-4702 ext 212
www.ci.niles.mi.us/Community/FortStJosephMuseum/ArcheologicalDig.htm

Beginning in 1691, Fort St. Joseph existed for 90 years, and it is one of the oldest forts on the continent. It existed when the area was in a state of flux and control of the land shifted dramatically. Originally American Indian land, the Indian land shifted to French, British, Canadian and United States control. Now it is an archaeological project that has given real vitality and excitement to the St. Joseph Museum. A unique partnership exists between Western Michigan University and the City of Niles, allowing for historical research and public education. This site, often covered by water from the river, is part of the museum's Open House—call for the dates and times. The Open House features costumed re-enactors and lots of events for the family. The museum is in an old carriage house and focuses on the story of Niles. It is part of the Underground Railroad, as well as the earlier stages of colonial history.

8 Freedom Trail

http://mi.gov/dnr/0,1607,7-153-54463_54465_45184---,00.html
www.adventurecycling.org/ugrr/

Some stories cannot be captured in a single exhibit or a video. Instead, you need a personal connection, and it takes some effort to begin to comprehend the full extent of the story. This is true of the Freedom Trail, which is known more often as the Underground Railroad. This highly charged and emotional story is about the flight from slavery. Imagine traveling by night and hiding in basements and outbuildings while trying to escape from men with guns, whips and dogs. This is a terrible part of the story of the United States, but one that must be told. The stories of those courageous slaves who fled—and the tales of the people who sheltered them—are too often forgotten. Unfortunately, it's difficult to trace the physical route of the Freedom Trail, so it's often best to start by visiting the museums listed in this section. If you want to begin a personal investigation of the actual trail, a bicycling group has mapped a route that is an ideal place to start. The route passes through many states and moves through Detroit to Canada. The route can be taken by car, as well as by bike.

9 Greenfield Village

20900 Oakwood Blvd., Dearborn; (800) 835-5237
www.hfmgv.org/

Pair this village experience with the Henry Ford Museum and you will have at least one full day of learning and fun. As this site demonstrates, history is anything but boring. With special events, such as the War of 1812 Muster and a number of car shows, the village is constantly changing and worth revisiting. Even so, the basic experience is so well done that it stands alone without the extras. From the Model T rides and historic horse-drawn carriages and motorized buses to sites like Thomas Edison's laboratory, Lincoln's courthouse, and the Wright Brothers' cycle shop, the village brings history to life. This is a complete village, not just isolated buildings, and the costumed actors here help make the time travel even more real.

10 Keweenaw National Historical Park

25970 Red Jacket Rd, Calumet 49913; (906) 483-3176
www.nps.gov/kewe/

Copper mining is the focus of this national historical park, but there's a lot more to see here, including lighthouses, nature preserves and charming communities. All of these sites are intertwined in a driving

tour. The park offers excellent exhibits and stories in their National Park Service's Calumet Visitor Center, and it also serves as a tour information center linking the mining tours, museums and historic sites so you can maximize your time and exploration. The Keweenaw Heritage Sites, non-federal partners of the Keweenaw National Historical Park, are privately owned and aspire to meet the high standards of the National Park Service. There are more than 25 such heritage sites throughout Houghton, Keweenaw, Baraga and Ontonagon Counties. There is also a seasonal visitor center open during summer at the Quincy Mine & Hoist.

11 Michigan Historical Museum

702 W Kalamazoo St, Lansing 48915; (517) 373-1359
www.michigan.gov/museum/

When it comes to teaching kids about history, interactive exhibits are key, and this museum has exhibits that will draw in visitors of any age. As one commented, "I didn't know Michigan had so much history." Well, it does, and the five levels of the Michigan Historical Museum cover all of it, from prehistory to the present day. At the beginning of the museum, there is a 3-story relief map of Michigan, and as a map person, I found it almost hard to leave. Even so, there's much more to see—you'll want to see how the museum re-created a copper mine from the U.P. and depicts the stories of the L.P.

12 Port Huron Museum

1115 Sixth Street, Port Huron 48060; (810) 982-0891
www.phmuseum.org/drupal/

The Port Huron Museum is a great place to take the entire family. You can explore the beautiful Blue Water Area on one of their surreys, cruisers or tandem bikes, located at the Thomas Edison Depot Museum. Rent for an hour or day and explore along the boardwalk, take the trails to historic downtown or stop at several of their museums nearby. The Thomas Edison Depot (built in 1858) is the actual structure where Thomas Edison worked from 1859–63, pedaling news to passengers riding the train between Port Huron and Detroit. Step inside the depot and discover his chemistry lab and printing shop. Reopened in May 2012, the Fort Gratiot Light Station is only a few pedals away. Tour the oldest lighthouse tower in Michigan, built in 1829, located on 5 acres and adjacent to Lake Huron. Looking for a place to take your family, or your church or scouting group? Book an overnight in the renovated duplex next to the lighthouse. Just a short distance away is the historic Huron Lightship, which was built in 1920 and became a National Historic Landmark in 1989. The Lightship was the last floating lighthouse on the Great Lakes. Be sure to save time for the Carnegie Center Museum, built in 1904 and funded by Andrew Carnegie. The building is as historic as the exhibits inside.

13 River Raisin National Battlefield Park & Visitor Center

1403 E Elm Ave, Monroe; (734) 243-7136
www.riverraisinbattlefield.org/visitorscenter.htm

This is one of the newest additions to the National Park System's battlefield collection. Most of us do not know much about the War of 1812, but it was an important war and this battle was a big one. There were 934 Americans who fought here and only 33 who were not killed or captured. People who play simulated war games will love the diorama; other exhibits will help describe both the battle and the context of the war. The visitor center claims that the 14-minute fiber optic map is the highlight of the interpretive presentations, but you need to go and see just for yourself how this high tech demonstration tells the story.

14 Sanilac Petroglyphs Historic State Park

8251 Germania Rd, Cass City 48726; (989) 856-4411
www.michigandnr.com/parksandtrails/Details.aspx?id=490&type=SPRK

Sanilac Petroglyphs Historic State Park has the Lower Peninsula's only known petroglyphs. A petroglyph is carved into rock—a pictograph is painted on rock. A hiking trail allows access to the artwork, as well as crossing the Little Cass River. The story of discovery involves a forest fire in 1881 that exposed the sandstone rocks. These carvings are somewhere between 300–1,000 years old and are subject to erosion because the rock is soft. The website describes the designs as "swirls, lines, handprints, flying birds and bow-wielding men." Respect the history and help preserve these messages from the past. Viewing has been limited to the weekends.

Mackinac Island

You don't need to go to the Caribbean to have an island getaway. The cool waters of the Great Lakes surround some of the most interesting islands in the world. Here you can find everything from a nineteenth-century getaway to remote wilderness landscapes. If you don't have a boat, that's no problem; there are numerous ferries to some of the more popular locations and bridges to others. If you have a boat, even more remote adventures await. But no matter what, don't put off your island-hopping, as there's simply so much to see.

ISLAND DESTINATIONS

1 Beaver Islands

Beaver Island Chamber of Commerce, PO Box 5, Beaver Island 49782;
(231) 448-2505
http://beaverisland.org/

Claimed to be the most remote of the Great Lakes' inhabited islands, Beaver Island is the largest island in Lake Michigan. Home to a population of 650 people of mostly Irish descent. The island has a strange history. In part because of its remoteness, a Mormon man named James Strang declared the islands a monarchy and named himself king. After his death, a wave of Irish immigrants moved to the islands. These stories are now a fascinating part of Michigan lore. Today, the islands are a destination for those seeking the quiet of nature. Home to 11 remote lighthouses, many people like to tour the islands by boat or plane. Located 32 miles from Charlevoix, you can get to the Islands by Island Airways and Fresh Air Aviation or via the Beaver Island Boat Company (which offers auto ferry service from Charlevoix). Driving, biking and hiking are the best ways to explore the island.

2 Drummond Island

Drummond Island Tourism Association, PO Box 200, Drummond Island 49726;
(906) 493-5245, (800) 737-8666
www.drummondisland.com/

Located only 1 mile from the eastern tip of Michigan's U.P., a quick glance at the map might lead you to think this is just part of the peninsula, but once you discover the truth you will be treated to a real island experience. Visitors can reach the island by plane or boat, or they will bring along their car or snowmobile, thanks to the auto ferry from DeTour Village. Once you're there, there's much to do. Like on many of Michigan's islands, there is a wonderful lighthouse to explore here, the DeTour Reef Light. Visitors to the island often enjoy bird watching or fishing in the inland lakes. A state forest campground and the Drummond Island Township Park provide primitive camping facilities. Boat owners will also find a full-service marina. If you do not have your own boat, there are charter services for touring and fishing. You will also find a few stores for supplies, a golf course, and snowmobile rentals in the winter.

3 Grand Island National Recreation Area

Munising Ranger District, 400 E Munising Ave, Munising 49862; (906) 387-2512,
(906) 387-3700
Grand Island Ferry Service, N8016 Grand Island Landing Rd, Munising 49862;
(906) 387-3503
http://grandislandmi.com/

How can such a large island be a hidden gem? This island features
300-foot cliffs, forest, inland lakes, and even an abandoned lighthouse,
but the island is easy to access because of convenient ferry service.
Once there, you can explore the island by trail or bike, and with a
boat you can explore the wild and dramatic shoreline. There are also
campsites and fishing opportunities, but mountain biking might be the
most popular island experience. Sea kayaking is also a popular way to
explore the island. Just be prepared, because this is a wilderness island
without support facilities.

4 Isle Royale

Isle Royale National Park, 800 E Lakeshore Dr, Houghton 49931-1896;
(906) 482-0984
www.nps.gov/isro/index.htm

This is a wilderness island and one of the most magnificent and rugged
islands in Lake Superior. The second-largest Great Lakes island and the
largest in Lake Superior, Isle Royale is approximately 45 miles long and
8.5 miles across and contains roughly 165 miles of trails. Isle Royale is
actually part of an archipelago with 450 islands, 110 of which are
named. If you're visiting but don't want to camp in the wilderness, you
can stay in facilities at Rock Harbor, where you can enjoy ranger
presentations, visit the research area at Daisy Farm Area, join tours to
Edison Fishery, take a guided tour to Passage Island Lighthouse or
Hidden Lake/Lookout Louise, take a cruise to Minong Mine, or enjoy
the sunset at Raspberry Island.

5 Les Cheneaux Islands

Les Cheneaux Islands Area Tourist Association, PO Box 422, 680 W M-134,
Cedarville 49719;
www.lescheneaux.org/

Mackinac Island is not the only island in the Straits of Mackinac.
Thirty-six islands are found in the shadow of the famous island, and
replete with channels and bays, they deserve much more attention
than they receive. Roughly translated, "Les Cheneaux" means "the
channels" in French, and that describes the sheltered waters that await
recreational boaters. Here visitors can find giant forests, miles of trails,

and sheltered marinas that serve as the perfect places to begin your fishing expeditions and exploration of Lake Huron. The islands are so biologically rich that The Nature Conservancy and the Little Traverse Conservancy have protected many reserves. None of the islands are developed; most are not even recommended destinations, but sailing and kayaking along these islands remains an inspiring experience. And not to be outdone by the wilds, the communities on the mainland closest to the islands also provide entertainment, such as the Antique Wooden Boat Show at Hessel. The town of Cedarville is home to the Great Lakes Boat Building School. It is the only boat-building school in the Midwest and is open year-round to visitors by land or water.

6 Mackinac Island

(800) 454-5227, (906) 847-3783
www.mackinacisland.org/
www.mackinacparks.com/

There are many reasons Mackinac Island is the most famous island in the Great Lakes. Located near the strait that separates Lakes Huron and Michigan, this island is a veritable time capsule and one that continues to provide memorable experiences for all ages. Cars are banned on the island, so travel is limited to bikes, horse and buggy, and walking, so the pace is nice and slow for everyone. With great restaurants and lodges this could easily be made into more than a day trip, but a 1-day trip is possible. However, if you're making it a 1-day trip, make sure to focus your visit, as there is simply too much to do here. The following activities are especially popular:

Explore the state park, Fort Mackinac and participate in activities
Visit the butterfly house
Try the world-famous Mackinac Island fudge
Tour the historic Grand Hotel
Ride a bicycle around the island
Visit the Mackinac Art Museum
Ride in a carriage tour
Visit Arch Rock and Skull Cave
Listen to music in the park during summer
Enjoy the annual horse parade

7 North and South Manitou Islands

Sleeping Bear Dunes National Lakeshore, 9922 Front St, Empire 49630;
(231) 326-5134
Provides ferry service: www.manitoutransit.com/
www.northmanitou.com
www.nps.gov/slbe/planyourvisit/northmanitouisland.htm
www.nps.gov/slbe/planyourvisit/southmanitouisland.htm

With a magnificent shoreline and giant sand dunes to grab your attention, you can be forgiven for not thinking of islands when you plan your trip to Sleeping Bear Dunes National Lakeshore. Nevertheless, the lakeshore includes 2 magnificent islands and both are worthy of a visit. As a matter of fact, the cruise can be a sunset happy hour or you can stay on the island for your camping pleasure. North Manitou is managed as a wilderness except for a 27-acre area around a small historic village. South Manitou is also uninhabited, but the trails go through old farm fields as well as natural landscapes. In previous centuries, the island provided one of the only harbors on Lake Michigan's eastern shore and a fueling station with a lighthouse. Ancient white cedars are one of the most significant plants on the island, and the surrounding waters include numerous shipwrecks. If you pack a lunch, you can take the ferry for a 1-day visit, but an overnight stay is a welcome way to experience both islands. No services are available.

Island Destinations

The Lighthouse Museum near the Mackinac Bridge

Over its history, Michigan has had more than 150 lighthouses—more than any other state. Lighthouses may no longer be staffed by lighthouse keepers, but they have lost none of their charm, and they still serve as beacons for ships and tourists alike.

LIGHTHOUSES

1 40 Mile Point Lighthouse

Presque Isle County's Lighthouse Park, 7 miles north of Rogers City;
(989) 734-4587
http://40milepointlighthouse.org/

This lighthouse, built in 1896, is 40 miles southeast of Mackinac
Point and 40 miles northwest of Thunder Bay, so the name is logical
if you are navigating the lake. When you visit, take a look around
the lighthouse and enjoy its fabulous swath of beach. We enjoyed
the vista, but we were also struck by the lighthouse's odd placement;
unlike most lighthouses, it isn't located near a point or a stream. 40
Mile Light was placed here to fill a void between lighthouses and to
make sure navigators could see a lighthouse on their entire journey
along this shore.

2 Au Sable Light Station— Pictured Rocks National Lakeshore

Pictured Rocks National Lakeshore, PO Box 40, Munising 49862-0040;
(906) 387-3700, (906) 494-2660 (summer only)
12 miles west of Grand Marais on Alger Co Rd H-58
Tours are offered Memorial Day to Labor Day
www.nps.gov/piro/historyculture/ausablelightstation.htm

Pictured Rocks National Lakeshore appears in many sections of this
book. There are many options for a day trip, one of which is the Au
Sable Light Station. Built in 1874, it is a tall white tower that rises
high above the lake and sits amid a complex of buildings. The 3-mile
round-trip walk to Au Sable Light Station is a very pleasant hike,
both on the old roadbed and along the shore. From the shore you
can see portions of old shipwrecks, reminders of why the lighthouse
was built. When you visit, take a tour guided by a park ranger to
maximize your experience.

3 Big Sable Point Lighthouse

8800 W M-116, Ludington 49431; (231) 843-2423
www.visitludingtonstatepark.com/stories/big_sable_point_lighthouse_luding-
ton_state_park_lake_michigan

Big Sable Point Lighthouse (1867) has a black-and-white tower with
a 130-foot stairway that winds up to the Fresnel light. A group of

volunteers dedicated to the legacy of lighthouses leads guided tours of the lighthouse and shares its stories. As part of a state park full of beaches and dunes, the lighthouse tour can be combined with many activities and could be incorporated into a walking or biking adventure.

4 Copper Harbor Light

US 41, Copper Harbor 49918
www.copperharborlighthouse.com/index.html

The Copper Harbor Light (1848) is located on a peninsula in the harbor and provides both beautiful scenery and a boating adventure you can tour. The Navy motor whale boat that the tour operators use is the kind of boat that the early lighthouse keepers would have used. The tour provides good opportunities for photography as well as a sense of history. Along with Whitefish Point Light Station, this was the first light tower constructed on Lake Superior. The keeper's house is maintained by Fort Wilkins Historic State Park and restored to conditions as found in 1866.

5 Crisp Point Lighthouse

Crisp Point Light Historical Society, 450 W Marr Rd, Howell 48855;
(517) 230-6294
http://crisppointlighthouse.org/

Crisp Point Light is one of our favorite lighthouses; it was a highlight on our walk around Lake Superior and has the classic form we all associate with lighthouses. The lighthouse is located in the northeast corner of Luce County.

Crisp Point Lighthouse became operational on May 5, 1904, and it was then situated on a point, which since has disappeared. In 1965, the Coast Guard destroyed the support structures around the light and it was in 1992 that the Crisp Point Light Historical Society was formed by Don and Nellie Ross of Ohio to preserve the light.

Now the lighthouse stands on a long length of sand beach, a beacon to hikers and boaters and a destination for lighthouse lovers. You can drive to the lighthouse, which is open from 10 a.m. to 5 p.m. from mid-May through early October when volunteers are on hand. A visit should include time to explore the beach.

6 Eagle Harbor Lighthouse Complex and Museum

400-404 Lighthouse Rd, Mohawk 49950
www.keweenawhistory.org/Sites/Lighthouse.html

Built in 1851, the red brick Eagle Harbor Lighthouse Complex and Museum is designated a Heritage Site of the Keweenaw National

Historical Park. Copper mining on the peninsula led to more shipping, and this octagonal light was built. The harbor is rock lined and dangerous in any weather, so the light was used to guide the ships past the natural reefs and on to the copper mines. When you visit this station, check out the restored Life Saving Station and the fishing museum in the assistant keeper's house. Because this harbor is located so far north, it is exposed to dangerous storms and large waves.

7 Fort Gratiot Lighthouse

(810) 982-0891 ext 110
www.huroncountyparks.com/page9.php
www.phmuseum.org/drupal/about/fortgratiotlighthouse

Lake Huron's shores are dotted with lighthouses, and Fort Gratiot is one of the oldest. First established in 1814, the light was built in 1825, but it collapsed a few years later. The new one was built in 1829. The lighthouse tower is open for observing the lakeshore, and a nearby museum provides history of the site. Very few original lights still exist, but that does not diminish their history and story. Like a few other lighthouses on this list, there is an active Coast Guard station nearby.

8 Grand Traverse Lighthouse

Grand Traverse Lighthouse Museum, 15500 N Lighthouse Point Rd, PO Box 43, Northport 49670; (231) 386-7195
www.grandtraverselighthouse.com/

At the tip of Leelanau Peninsula, a visit to the Grand Traverse Lighthouse (built in 1852) is a great addition to your wine-tasting adventures on the Leelanau Peninsula, which is home to more than a dozen wineries. The lighthouse itself marks the beginning of Grand Traverse Bay. When it comes to its name, you might encounter a bit of confusion, as locals might call this Cathead Light or Northport Light. Whatever you call it, like most of Michigan's lighthouses, the original structure no longer stands. When the lighthouse was active, it was constantly upgraded to provide the most effective service; like many other lighthouses, it was restored after it was decommissioned. The Grand Traverse Lighthouse was restored to how it looked in the '20s and '30s.

9 Lighthouse Museum

526 N Huron Ave, Mackinaw City 49701; (231) 436 4100
www.mackinacparks.com/old-mackinac-point-lighthouse/

Looking like a sturdy house as much as a lighthouse, this museum lighthouse is on the shore next to the Mackinac Bridge and is part of the Mackinac State Park complex. At the point where Lakes Michigan and Huron meet, this was an important light during the early days of shipping and remains an impressive building that defies the northern winter. As nice as the inside is, the view from the top is probably the most impressive part of the lighthouse, and it is definitely worth stopping to check out. The light operated from 1890 to 1958.

10 Marquette Harbor Lighthouse and Maritime Museum

300 Lakeshore Blvd., Marquette 49855; (906) 226-2006
https://www.mqtmaritimemuseum.com/

This square red lighthouse is the signature building of the Marquette harbor. The Maritime Museum, housed in a classic sandstone building—Old City Waterworks—is a collection of artifacts and stories about local lighthouses, Fresnel lenses, shipwrecks, and lighthouse keepers. In this small hidden gem, there are also stories about American Indians, fishermen and commercial shipping. The museum sits beside an active Coast Guard station, a reminder of the perils of navigating on the Great Lakes.

11 New and Old Presque Isle Lighthouses

5295 E Grand Lake Rd, Presque Isle; (989) 595-6979,
New Presque Isle Lighthouse, 4500 E Grand Lake Rd, Presque Isle;
(989) 595-9917
www.presqueisletwp.org
www.presqueislelighthouses.org/

If you're keeping track of all the lighthouses you see, you can add 2 lighthouses on this visit. The Presque Isle Light Station, built in 1870, is the tallest tower open to the public and the view is great, but so is the sensation of being on the narrow walkway outside the light. As you might expect, the 1905 keeper's house is now a museum. We brought a picnic and enjoyed the shore and the grounds, as well as the light. The old lighthouse dates back to 1840 and is less impressive until you take into account its age and the tools they had to work with when the hand-hewn stone steps were created.

12 Point Betsie Lighthouse

The Friends of Point Betsie Lighthouse, PO Box 601, Frankfort 49635-0601; (231) 352-7644
www.pointbetsie.org/

All the Great Lakes have lighthouses along their shorelines and we are fortunate they were not mass-produced in one style. It is the variations that give them so much charm and enhance the landscape. Located on the southern entrance to Manitou Passage, the Point Betsie Lighthouse (active 1857–1937) is just south of Sleeping Bear Dunes National Lakeshore and a nice addition to other adventures in the area. There was also a rescue station associated with the light.

13 Point Iroquois Lighthouse

Brimley, where M-221 dead-ends at Lake Superior; (906) 437-5272

From Whitefish Point to Point Iroquois Lighthouse, ships continue into the St. Marys River and the Soo Locks. The narrowing of the lake at the mouth of the river can create turbulent conditions. Point Iroquois light was just one of the important signals that have been put in place since the canal opened in 1855. The lighthouse and tower are in excellent shape and open for tours. The name of the lighthouse and the point comes from a battle fought in 1662 with the Iroquois Indians. The resident Ojibwa were able to defeat the Iroquois. The area around the lighthouse is sheltered and provides access to a beautiful and peaceful beach, with boardwalks through the sensitive dune area.

14 Pointe aux Barques Lighthouse

Pointe aux Barques Lighthouse Society, Lighthouse County Park, 7320 Light-house Rd, Port Hope 48468
http://pointeauxbarqueslighthouse.org/

The original Pointe aux Barques Lighthouse was built of stone and rock from the surrounding Lake Huron shore, and with this structure was a detached 28-foot tower. By 1857, the tower had deteriorated so badly that it was condemned. The new keeper's house with an attached 89-foot tower was completed the same year and the beacon has been in continuous operation since that date. The Life Saving

Station was opened in 1875 (the first one on the Great Lakes) and operated until decommissioned in 1937. This group was credited with more than 200 rescues in an area considered one of the most dangerous on the Lakes. The keeper's home has become a museum filled with lighthouse, Great Lakes and Huron County history, all available free of charge.

15 Sturgeon Point Lighthouse

Harrisville 48740; (989) 727-4703
www.dnr.state.mi.us/parksandtrails/Details.aspx?id=498&type=SPRK

Protecting ships from a shallow reef in Lake Huron, Sturgeon Point Lighthouse has been in continuous operation since 1870 and is used by recreational as well as commercial vessels. Serious lighthouse observers will recognize this as a Cape Cod-style lighthouse, just one example of the many lighthouse styles found in the state. Volunteers have restored the keeper's house and turned it into a museum. If you look just offshore as you admire the lighthouse, you can see the reason the lighthouse was built: the reef just below the surface. Just to the north is an area known as Sanctuary Bay, a place of safety for ships trying to get to calmer waters. This light is within a Michigan state park.

16 Whitefish Point Light Station

Great Lakes Shipwreck Museum, 18335 N Whitefish Point Rd, Paradise 49768; (888) 492-3747
www.shipwreckmuseum.com/whitefish-point-4/

This lighthouse (in service since 1849) is connected with the Great Lakes Shipwreck Museum and also is next to the Whitefish Point Bird Observatory, making a visit here one of the most enjoyable and diverse days for lighthouse fans. Located on a beautiful spit of land and a crucial point in navigation, this lighthouse may be beautiful, but it's also important—it is close to the site where the *Edmund Fitzgerald* went down. It is a fascinating part of history, and along with the keeper's house, it makes for a very accessible destination.

Mineral stained cliffs of Pictured Rocks

Michigan is a land of contrasts, and rock hounds can enjoy this variety by wandering beaches and collecting agates and Petoskey stones, taking tours of iron and copper mines, and taking in the colorful scenery of Pictured Rocks National Lakeshore. At Pictured Rocks, there are patterns in the sandstones and limestones unlike those found anywhere else. With all this and more, Michigan has much to offer visitors interested in rock hounding, mining or geology.

ROCKS & MINERALS

1 A. E. Seaman Mineral Museum

Michigan Technological University, 1404 E Sharon Ave, Houghton 49931-1295;
(906) 487-2572
www.museum.mtu.edu/

Leave it to a Michigan university to pull together the most gorgeous collection of Michigan minerals. Whether they are metallic, fluorescent or fossils, these specimens are works of art, but they also tell stories. If the mining tours have sparked your interest in rocks and minerals, then this museum has what you need. Named after a geology professor, this museum houses 25,000-plus specimens, most of which represent the Lake Superior region. That, in itself, tells you how complex the geology of this region really is.

2 Cliff Shafts Mine Museum

PO Box 555, Ishpeming 49849; (906) 485-1882
www.me.mtu.edu/~jdschust/cliffs/main.html

Iron mining in the U.P. dates back to the mid-1800s. Just after the Civil War, the Cliff Shafts began to produce ore, but it wasn't until 1919 that the mine gained its claim to fame: the massive obelisks that are now placed in front of the A and B shafts. These obelisks came into being when the old wooden frames needed replacing. The company decided that the new structure would make an architectural statement. The famous architect, George Washington Maher, designed a 97-foot-tall concrete Egyptian Revival obelisk to be placed at both the A and B shafts. These obelisks became a symbol of Ishpeming itself. Mining ceased in 1967, but today the site is preserved for the visiting public. Its many artifacts and unique stories help convey the unique history of the area.

3 Collecting Petoskey Stones

Little Traverse Bay stony beaches and gravel areas
www.petoskeyarea.com/petoskey-stone-73/

With all the great museums in Michigan, there are many treasures, but sometimes you have to do some treasure hunting of your own. Near Little Traverse Bay and all of its shops, trails and restaurants, a small stone is the elusive prize. Petoskey stones are fossils of small corals (*Hexagonaria percarinata*) that lived during the Devonian period (360 million years ago). Much later, these fossils were scattered around the area by glaciers. As their scientific name suggests, hexagon patterns mark the coral and give it the distinctive quality that collectors love. Finding Petoskey stones on Michigan's rocky beaches is fun and rewarding, and while it can be difficult to spot them, searching for them is a popular pastime. In fact, the Petoskey stone is so popular that it was named the state stone of Michigan in 1965. If you can't find them yourself, Petoskey stones are found in jewelry stores, gift shops and museums. And if you like this kind of adventure, you can always attend the annual Petoskey Stone Festival.

4 Coppertown Mining Museum

Coppertown USA Mining Museum, Red Jacket Rd, Calumet 49913;
(906) 337-4354
www.uppermichigan.com/coppertown/

Copper is a precious metal that is in great demand. It can often be found in very pure concentrations, but the history of copper mining in Michigan dates back to American Indians, who collected exposed copper and dug trenches to expose underground copper veins. They beat the copper, shaped it, and used it for a number of purposes. Eventually, men like David Houghton traveled to Lake Superior's wild shoreline in search of mineral wealth. There, they occasionally found huge boulders of copper, such as the Ontonagon Boulder (which weighed nearly 2 tons). In subsequent years, miners and engineers learned how to extract the ore from the ground more efficiently. In so doing, towns were built, lives were lost, and a rich history was written. With artifacts and well-constructed exhibits, Coppertown Mining Museum tells the story of Michigan's long mining history.

5 Delaware Copper Mine Tours

US 41, 12 miles south of Copper Harbor; (906) 289-4688
http://delawarecopperminetours.com/

One of the earliest mines in the Keweenaw Peninsula, the Delaware Copper Mine operated from 1847–87 and produced 8 million pounds of copper. Today's visitors can take a self-guided tour of the mine's first level, 100 feet below the surface, to see where American copper mining began. Pure veins of copper are exposed in the walls, along with other geological interests. Aboveground, walking trails pass mine ruins, antique engines, trains, and animal pens. A prehistoric mining pit is also located on the grounds. Stop in the gift shop and visit our pet skunks. Pets are welcome on our tours, too! Delaware Copper Mine is a Heritage Site of the Keweenaw National Historical Park.

6 Keweenaw National Historical Park

Visitor Center, 89th Fifth St, Calumet 49913; (906) 483-3178
Open Memorial Day–Labor Day, 9 a.m. til 5 p.m. 7 days a week, off-season as
staffing permits
www.nps.gov/kewe/

It is hard to explain Keweenaw National Historical Park. Unlike other
parks, it does not own all of the resources that it encompasses. It's a
collaborative park, one where the Park Service partners with existing
tour operators and even historic communities (such as Calumet) to
tell a regional story of national importance. Think of the entire
Keweenaw as the park dedicated to the history of copper mining.
Nonetheless, this park isn't just about mining; it's also about people,
as you'll learn about the Finnish and Cornish immigrants, who were
the primary workforce of the mines. To get started, head to the
Calumet Visitor Center near downtown Calumet; it has information
about what to see, exhibits, historic photos, as well as a gift shop.

7 Lake Superior Agates

Lake Superior's shoreline and the glacial gravel deposits
www.treasurehuntingplaces.com/banded-agates/lake-superior-agates/

Over a billion years ago, an immense amount of lava cooled in what
would become the Lake Superior basin. As this lava cooled, volcanic
gases were trapped in the lava, forming small cavities. Eventually,
silica-infused water seeped into these cavities, leading to the formation
of Lake Superior agates. These popular gemstones exhibit concentric
or parallel banding and are often tinted in rich hues of red and brown.
Millions of years after the agates formed, glaciers bulldozed their way
across the region, uncovering the long-buried agates and transporting
them across a wide area. Since then, water and waves have washed
these stones and further distributed them, and they can be found on
rocky shores and at gravel pits. Agates are smooth and hard and polish
to a brilliant sheen. In fact, that's one way to spot them. When you're
hunting, look for rocks that are glassy and reflect light. In the L.P., you
can find agates where you find Petoskey stones. One last thing, don't
say we didn't warn you: agate hunting is addictive.

8 | Menominee Range Historical Museum

300 E Ludington St, Iron Mountain 49801; (906) 774-4276
www.menomineemuseum.com/
Cornish Pumping Engine & Mining Museum, 300 Kent St, Iron Mountain 49801;
(906) 774-1086
www.menomineemuseum.com/cornishpump.html

Named for the Menominee River, which separates the U.P. from
northeastern Wisconsin, the mineral-rich Menominee Iron Range
covers an area from eastern Dickinson County, Michigan, through
Florence County, Wisconsin, and up through Iron County, Michigan
The Menominee Range Historical Museum, located in the former
Carnegie Public Library, is listed as a Michigan Historic Site and
features more than 100 exhibits depicting local history, from American
Indian inhabitants to the early twentieth century, with chronological
displays and re-created period rooms. The Cornish Pumping Engine &
Mining Museum features the largest standing steam-driven pumping
engine ever built in the United States and one of the largest pumping
engines in the world. Mining collectors and history buffs alike will find
it to be of special interest. Both museums are operated by the Menominee Range Historical Foundation.

9 | Michigan Historical Museum

702 W Kalamazoo St, Lansing 48915; (517) 373-3559
www.michigan.gov/museum/

When telling the story of a state's history, it is logical to begin with its
geology, and that's especially true in a mineral-rich state like Michigan,
where mining has played such an important role. This museum
features five stories of exhibits and artifacts, and attempts to cover the
whole of Michigan's history. But pay particular attention to the exhibits
about minerals and mining, as they are fascinating. Our mining gallery
includes a huge piece of float copper and a mine. If you would like to
learn more about what is in the mining gallery, please visit www.hal.
state.mi.us/mhc/museum/explore/museums/hismus/prehist/mining/
index.html.

10 | Michigan Iron Industry Museum

73 Forge Rd, Negaunee 49866; (906) 475-7857
www.michigan.gov/dnr/0,1607,7-153-54463_18595_18611---,00.html7
www.michigan.gov/dnr/0,4570,7-153-54463_18595_18611-54393--,00.html

This museum is fascinating because of both its content and its location
on the Carp River Forge. The site is beautiful, but it is also a reminder
of what the landscape looked like before mining. Inside, the exhibits
tell the story of mining and also the story of the miners themselves.

Rocks &
Minerals

The miners worked hard under difficult conditions, but the wealth generated by the mines didn't flow back to them. These were people who sacrificed, but survived. Their stories are fascinating, and so is the history of mining and the advancement of mining technology.

11 Old Victoria

PO Box 43, Rockland 49960-0043; (906) 886-2617
www.oldvictoria.net/

At Old Victoria, you can get a closer look at the day-to-day lives of miners and their families. While the miners spent all day in the ground, their families had their cabins, but that, too, was a confinement. Like other mining towns, the town of Victoria offered products but not a lot more. Couple the cabins with the ruins, and it feels almost like a ghost story. With abandoned homes and relics still on the ground, sites like these have a different feel than designed exhibits. You can almost hear an echo of the past as you look at these remnants of past lives.

12 Petoskey Stone Festival

Barnes Park, PO Box 504, Eastport 49627; (231) 599-2712
www.petoskeystonefestival.com/

Each year in Eastport, the Petoskey Stone Festival features Michigan's state stone. Petoskey stones are fossilized small corals (*Hexagonaria percarinata*) from the Devonian period (360 million years ago). Much later, glaciers scattered these fossils around the area. As the scientific name suggests, hexagon patterns mark the corals and give them the distinctive quality that collectors love.

13 Pictured Rocks National Lakeshore

PO Box 40, Munising 49862-0040
Interagency Visitor Center (year-round), 400 E Munising Ave, Munising 49862; (906) 387-3700
Grand Sable Visitor Center (summer only), E21090 Co Rd H-58, Grand Marais; (906) 494-2660
www.nps.gov/piro/

Pictured Rocks National Lakeshore is home to mineral-stained rocks, cliffs, waves and water. These naturally sculptured wonders also tell an important geological story. As you walk through the trails and explore the layered rocks, you can walk past rocks that differ widely in age, from rocks from the late Precambrian period (570 million years ago) to those from the early Ordovician period (505 million years ago). Then the geology makes a tremendous leap; instead of hundreds of millions of years old, the geological features are only thousands of years old, and there are glacial features to explore and try to understand. Each rock unit here has a different hardness, and this means each one weathers differently, leading to the celebrated shapes of the Pictured Rocks. Chapel Rock and Miners Castle are just a sample of the dramatic rock formations in the park.

14 Quincy Mine & Hoist, Mine and Tram

www.quincymine.com/

The Quincy Mine & Hoist is one of the most imposing and impressive sites near the towns of Houghton and Hancock. Like an ancient sculpture garden, this mine is set amid picturesque ruins from mining's heyday, and some of the mining artifacts look like large metal sculptures. Walking the ruins is fascinating, but going down the Quincy and Torch Lake Cog Railway to the mine is the most intriguing part of a visit. Like a good carnival ride, the tram has a steep grade and it may elicit a few screams from the kids (and the grandparents), but it delivers you safely to the mine entrance. Then the experience shifts: the dark shafts, artificial lights, and a tour guide will give you a feeling of what copper mining was like here from 1868 to 1920.

15 Tilden Mine Tours

4501 M-553, Marquette 49855; (888) 578-6489
www.miup.info/assets.asp?ait=av&aid=355

Unlike all the other tours in this section, the Tilden Mine is still producing ore, so you need verify that tours are available ahead of time. To visit the mine, you can catch the bus at the Iron Mining Museum in Negaunee, but make reservations, as this is very popular. If you are wondering why you would want to do this, consider the scale of the mine: it's 1 mile across and 1,200 feet deep. From the rim of the canyon, you can see trucks with 12-foot-high tires. If you were next to them, they'd look like monster trucks, but instead, they look like toys. Besides a visit to the pit itself, you will also get to enter the plant and learn about what happens when ore leaves the ground. The guides are employees of the iron mine and will share a personal perspective as they handle your questions.

The Air Zoo

When it comes to Michigan, cars, trucks and ships are undoubtedly the stars of the show, but they aren't the only ways to get around. Michigan also has an impressive history of air and rail travel, and these sites are great places to play and make for a wonderful day trip. In these places your travel will be both figurative and literal as you explore Michigan's rich transportation history.

RAILROADS & AIRPLANES

1 Air Zoo

6151 Portage Rd, Portage 49002; (269) 382-6555, (866) 524-7966
www.airzoo.org/

The Air Zoo doesn't give itself enough credit; this imaginative museum/amusement facility is not simply about aircraft. While it is home to a wonderful collection of airplanes and a great place to learn about the history of aviation (in both war and peace), this museum also features craft that ventured into space. Go to the Michigan Aviation Hall of Fame and gain an appreciation of the people who have connected us to outer space. You can walk around, observe, and take in the history that is here, but even better, get on the rides and have fun. If you've ever wanted to fly, try out the flight simulators. You can even sign up for real flight training through the Air Zoo.

2 Amtrak

Blue Water (364/365): Chicago to Port Huron
Pere Marquette (370/371): Chicago to Grand Rapids
Wolverine (350/351/352/353/354/355): Chicago to Pontiac
www.amtrak.com/michigan-services-train

Referred to as the Michigan Services, several Amtrak routes connect Michigan cities to Chicago and provide a relaxing way to see the scenic landscape. The service also restores the tradition of national parks and railroads that dates back to the nineteenth century in parks like Glacier and Yellowstone. Called the Trails & Rails program, Amtrak passengers taking the Wolverine route from Chicago, Illinois, to Niles, Michigan, will experience guided narration from the staff and volunteers of the Indiana Dunes National Lakeshore.

3 Little River Railroad— Coldwater to Quincy

Little River Railroad, 29 W Park Ave, Coldwater 49036
www.littleriverrailroad.com/

Even in this age of computers and jets, there is something romantic about railroads, not just the European and Japanese high-speed trains, but the old steam engines chugging along puffing white smoke into the blue sky. But steam engines aren't only found in history books; you can still catch a ride on one at the Little River Railroad, which runs between Coldwater and Quincy. The ride lasts 1½ hours, so climb on board and settle in. If you want more excitement, there are occasional train robbers, and strange as it might seem, they are held on schedule. Check out the railroad's other options that coincide with community events along the way.

4 Michigan Military and Space Museum

1250 Weiss St, Frankenmuth; (989) 652-8005
www.michigansmilitarymuseum.com/

If you are looking for history that is current and connected to your life, this is the place to go. Dedicated to honoring the efforts and stories of Michigan's 13 astronauts, 30 individual Medal of Honor recipients, and all of its governors, this museum tells a global story through the tales of individuals from Michigan. Everything from the Spanish–American War to the War on Terrorism is included here, and because the museum is located in popular Frankenmuth, it is easy to add to many different travel adventures.

5 Michigan Transit Museum

200 Grand Ave, Mount Clemens 48046; (586) 463-1863
Depot is open every Saturday and Sunday (except holidays) from 1–4 p.m.
Train runs at 1, 2, 3 and 4 p.m. every Sunday, June 1 through the end of October
www.michigantransitmuseum.org/

No railroad system could operate without depots, and that's especially true for passenger lines. This museum is located in the restored depot where Thomas Edison began his brief railroading career. Looking as pristine as it did in 1900, it holds displays from that same era, giving visitors both a sense of history and a feeling for what railroading was like. The depot was in use until 1980 and, while you can no longer catch a train from here, they will sell you tickets for a short ride that leaves from Joy Park on Sunday afternoons. A small museum and a short ride make for a perfect Sunday afternoon experience.

6 | Selfridge Military Air Museum

127 WG/MU
27333 C St, Bldg 1011, Selfridge ANG Base 48045; (586) 239-5035
www.selfridgeairmuseum.org/

This is an active military base that offers visitors weekend access. Here you can see a collection of restored military aircraft on display and a collection of exhibits that show the importance of airplanes throughout the military history of the United States. This is an outreach effort of the Michigan Air Guard Historical Association, and it honors this important branch of the Armed Forces. It also honors all those men and women who served America and lost their lives in their gallant efforts. It is both an inspiring and sobering history.

7 | Toonerville Trolley, River Boat and Train Ride to Tahquamenon Falls

Soo Junction; (888) 77-TRAIN, (888) 778-7246; Depot (906) 876-2311
www.superiorsights.com/toonerville/index.html

Now here is an idea: how about a 5½-hour train ride through the wild forests of the U.P., followed by a 21-mile riverboat ride to one of the nation's most beautiful waterfalls? The falls are located on the beautiful and wild Tahquamenon River. If you'd prefer to avoid the boat trip, you can choose to just do the railroad ride, but for a full-day trip, this is hard to beat. People have been taking this unusual tour since 1927, and the scenery and the stories continue to entertain and impress. Bear, moose, otters and migratory birds may make their appearances anywhere along the route, but you can always count on being cooled down by the mist of the falls.

Yankee Air Museum

Yankee Air Force Inc, 47884 D St, Belleville 48111-1126; (734) 483-4030
http://yankeeairmuseum.org/

If you did not know that Ford was once an airplane manufacturer, here is a fun way to learn a lot more about aviation. In 1941, this airfield was constructed to serve the B-24 bombers that were manufactured using Ford's mass-production techniques. At its height, the factory produced 1 bomber every 59 minutes. This museum and collection was devastated by fire in 2004, but the airplanes in flying condition were saved. Today their collection is world-famous and provides the visitor with great adventures. Come in, look around, and enjoy an air show, but if you want the most from your visit, book a flight on the B-17 *Yankee Lady* or B-25 *Yankee Warrior.*

Railroads & Airplanes

Ann Arbor Hands-on Museum

Michigan has a wonderful array of nature centers and museums that are devoted to connecting people with nature and helping visitors understand science. The great thing about these trips is that they aren't passive. You get to participate, both mentally and physically, and the result is a satisfying and fun experience.

SCIENCE MUSEUMS & NATURE CENTERS

1 Ann Arbor Hands-on Museum

220 E Ann St, Ann Arbor; (734) 995-5439
www.aahom.org/

If the key to learning is being engaged, then this museum will connect you and your family with science. This is a children's museum and a science center combined and a place to bring the family and to share experiences, ask questions, experiment and learn. The exhibits change over time, and many explore the concepts that are needed for more complex scientific inquiry. The exhibits cover such topics as weather, light, optics and bubbles, and there are plenty of other options when their interest for one topic wanes. If you aren't careful, you might just find that helping children learn teaches you, too.

2 Blandford Nature Center

1715 Hillburn Ave NW, Grand Rapids 49504; (616) 735-6240
www.blandfordnaturecenter.org/

An urban oasis that brings kids, families, and adults together, this nature center is home to a farm, trails and captive animals, and it hosts educational programs led by naturalists. The center consists of 143 acres in the middle of an urban area and features a visitor center, wildlife education center, agriculture, and 4 miles of trails, which give the visitor many options for a day of exploring or repeated visits. Like so many nature centers, this has become a refuge for injured wildlife that cannot be released into the wild. These animals supplement the natural diversity of the landscape and are an excellent way to help kids make connections with nature. To get the full flavor of the center, visit during all seasons, and don't forget to check out the seasonal events.

3 Chippewa Nature Center

400 S Badour Rd, Midland 48640-8661; (989) 631-0830
www.chippewanaturecenter.org/

Located across the river from downtown Midland, this nature center covers a varied landscape and includes part of the Chippewa Trail, so you can explore by both foot and bike. They also offer Nature

Preschool and a Nature Day Camp along with numerous special programs for adults and families.

A newly renovated visitor center is open seven days a week with free admission. Features include the Bur Oak Theater, where visitors can watch a series of short interpretive films, the River Overlook, with a stunning view of the Pine River, and the Wildlife Viewing Area, where spectators can watch the antics of animals at the feeders through one-way glass. The center also includes the hands-on Ecosystem Gallery and the hands-on, kid- friendly Nature Discovery area, which includes books, animal pelts, microscopes and more.

4 Cranbrook Institute of Science

39221 Woodward Ave, Bloomfield Hills 48303-0801; (248) 645-3200
http://science.cranbrook.edu/

This institute provides a great place to learn about science, technology, and natural history. There are well-designed exhibits, hands-on activities and planetarium shows, plus you can have a picnic or eat at the café to make this a day-long visit. Imagine a museum with dinosaurs, sparkling diamonds and a "Bat Zone." Here you can learn about the distant stars in the sky, or about bats close-up. A lecture series brings in experts who share their information, answer questions, and give visitors access to real scientists. The institute's programs vary by season, allowing the process of discovery to go on and on.

5 Curious Kids' Museum

415 Lake Blvd, St. Joseph 49085; (269) 983-2543
http://curiouskidsmuseum.org/

Science is serious, right? Well, yes and no. Science begins with fun, an invitation to explore and investigate, and the encouragement to experiment. Located on a bluff downtown that overlooks Lake Michigan, the Curious Kids' Museum is the place for kids to begin to learn about science. Each floor is filled with learning opportunities, games and exhibits, and your kids will give you laughs and insights with their play—but don't think that the fun ends when you leave the building. You can enjoy Silver Beach and the great Whirlpool Compass Fountain across the street or stroll along the bluff's History Trail. However, if you want to go all-out, the museum Discovery Zone Annex at Silver Beach Center is described as a place for "giggling, hopping, splashing, wiggling, st-r-r-e-e-t-ching, swirling and squeezing your way through an amazing world of science, history, technology and culture." The beach center is perfect for all kids, from toddlers to teens.

6 | **Dahlem Environmental Education Center**

The Dahlem Conservancy, 7117 S Jackson Rd, Jackson 49201; (517) 782-3453
www.dahlemcenter.org/

Located on nearly 300 acres, the Dahlem Center offers visitors 5 miles of walking trails to enjoy. The trails wander through a variety of habitats, from open grassland and oak savannas, to fens, ponds, woods and farmland. The visitor center is reached after a short stroll through gardens managed by the Jackson County Master Gardeners. The newly resurfaced Nature For All Trail provides an approximate quarter-mile nature experience for visitors with limited mobility (wheelchairs, walkers, strollers), and a new Nature Playscape offers free play opportunities for children of all ages in a safe environment. The property includes the Dahlem Ecology Farm, which features a 40-plot community garden and a public apiary. Dahlem is a wonderful place for birding and botanizing, and nature classes are offered year-round for adults, families and children.

7 | **Huron County Nature Center**

1005 Triangle Lake Rd, Howell 48843; (517) 546-0249
www.huronnaturecenter.org/

It's rare to find a piece of untouched land. And it's especially wonderful that a group way back in 1941 had the foresight to protect the land for future generations, but that is just what happened under the leadership of the Huron County Women's Club. In 1990, a new nature center was built here, where you can enjoy both the Wilderness Arboretum and events such as the Memorial Day weekend Lady's Slipper Festival. With alternating sand ridges (beaches) and shallow swales, this is a botanical treasure, and a place to discover the beauty of nature untrammeled.

8 Kalamazoo Nature Center

7000 N Westnedge Ave, Kalamazoo; (269) 381-1574
http://naturecenter.org/

Whether you want to learn about rural living and farms or experience nature and all its variations, this center is a treasure. Trained volunteers greet you as you enter and help you find the exhibits, the gift store, the programs, the trails, or the events that interest you. There are programs in all seasons. In addition, there are 11 miles of trails to wander. We recommend that you learn about the center's ties to national and regional scientific research and conservation efforts. In addition to being part of a national bird banding program called MAPS, the center is conducting important research about cerulean warblers.

9 Kalamazoo Valley Museum

230 N Rose St, Kalamazoo 49007; (800) 772-3370, (269) 373-7990
www.kalamazoomuseum.org/

This museum is the perfect place to get kids interested in science and history. Preschool-aged children can let their imaginations run wild in the Children's Landscape, a space specially designed for them. Older kids will love the Science Gallery, where they can build a car on the racetrack or learn firsthand how electricity powers everyday objects. Other permanent exhibits include favorites such as the "Kalamazoo Direct to You" history gallery and "Mystery of the Mummy," featuring a 2,300-year-old Egyptian mummy! Special traveling exhibits change often, so there's always something new to see and do. With tons of activities and hands-on interactivities, the Kalamazoo Valley Museum makes learning fun!

10 Sloan/Longway Museum and Planetarium

Sloan Museum, 1221 E Kearsley St, Flint 48503; (810) 237-3450
www.sloanlongway.org/SloanMuseum.aspx

If you want a high-quality museum that is also eclectic, this is your destination. There are several combined facilities here: the Buick Automotive Gallery, the Longway Planetarium, and the Sloan Museum. The museum covers a wide variety of subjects, including muscle cars, Sesame Street, and the history of the Girl Scouts, and displays change often. Of course, the Buick story is here, too, and shouldn't be missed. All of this variety makes it possible to enjoy a full day here.

11 Upper Peninsula Children's Museum

123 W Baraga Ave, Marquette 49855; (906) 226-3911
www.upchildrensmuseum.com/

When a setting is imaginative and engaging, play turns to learning. At this museum, there are many hands-on activities that cover everything from aviation to car mechanics and health and nutrition, and to how TV and radio broadcasts work. With such a variety, kids (and adults) can't help but have fun (and learn) at this museum.

12 Woldumar Nature Center

5739 Old Lansing Rd, Lansing 48917; (517) 322-0030
http://woldumar.org/

With 5 miles of trails, diverse ecosystems, and 1.25 miles bordering the Grand River, Woldumar Nature Center offers numerous options for hiking, cross-country skiing and bird watching, with a fantastic array of flora and fauna. The vast grounds include an herb garden, butterfly garden, native plant garden, and one of the oldest residences in Eaton County, the 1860 Moon Log Cabin. There are several special events at the center, including the American Heritage Festival in the fall, the annual 5K, 10K and Half Marathon Trail Run, the Chili Winter Evening, which features sleigh rides and a bowl of steaming chili, and a spring wildflower weekend.

Coaster II

When John Masefield wrote the famous lines, "I must go down to the seas again, to the lonely sea and the sky, / And all I ask is a tall ship and a star to steer her by," he might not have had Michigan in mind, but if he visited some of the exciting ship-related stops Michigan has to offer, he might have changed the line to, "I must go down to the lakes again." And, of course, if you're familiar with Michigan, you already know all about the Great Lakes, the allure of the sky, and the deep blue waters. Then again, maybe you're visiting because you've heard stories of Michigan's shipwrecks and ghost tales. If you have, then ships ahoy and welcome on board, matey!

SHIPS & SHIPWRECKS

1 Alpena Shipwreck Tours

500 W Fletcher St, Alpena; (888) 469-4696
Thunder Bay River is just behind the Great Lakes Maritime Heritage Center
Tickets are sold online at www.thunderbayfriends.org/ or at the Great Lakes
Maritime Heritage Center Museum Gift Store
www.alpenashipwrecktours.com/

This is Lake Huron's Shipwreck Alley and you can explore it and
see shipwrecks even if you don't scuba dive. Thunder Bay National
Marine Sanctuary sells tickets on the 65-foot-long *Lady Michigan*, a
tour boat with large "glass bottom" viewing wells. You can spend
2½ hours on the water learning about the ships, the shore, and the
lighthouses, and you can do so comfortably, with refreshments,
while away from Lake Huron's weather.

2 Appledore Tall Ships: Public Sails and Dinner Cruises

Appledore Tall Ships—BaySail, 107 5th St, Bay City 48708; (989) 895-5193
www.baysailbaycity.org/

The Appledore Tall Ships sail out of downtown Bay City and into
Saginaw Bay, where you can experience the thrill of setting sail
and catching the wind. You don't have to worry, though, as these
sailboats are supported by modern navigation and safety equipment,
so you can just participate and enjoy. There are private charters that
can be arranged or you can join the weekend public sails, which
also feature lunch and historical information. If you are looking for
something special, how about a Stargazer Sail on Saginaw River and
Huron's Saginaw Bay? If you still want something extra, consider
having a shipboard dinner and inquire about their extended sailing
expeditions. If you plan ahead, you can be onboard for the area's
annual fireworks festival.

3 Dossin Great Lakes Museum

100 Strand Dr, Belle Isle, Detroit 48207; (313) 833-5538
http://detroithistorical.org/dossin-great-lakes-museum/plan-your-visit/general-information

When you enter through the Gothic Room on this large ship, be prepared for opulence, which is probably not what you would expect from a shipping museum. The Gothic Room is the reconstructed gentlemen's lounge that existed on the *City of Detroit III*, when industrial giants rode this ship between Detroit and Cleveland or Buffalo. The museum is part of the Detroit Historical Museum group and also features the SS *William Clay Ford* pilot house. Here kids and adults can get a sense of what it might feel like to be in charge of one of the large vessels of the Great Lakes. The SS *William Clay Ford* was a 647-foot-long freighter that was built in 1952 and transported iron ore and coal to Ford's River Rouge Steel Plant. And don't miss the newly overhauled main exhibit, Built by the River (formerly City on the Straits), which discusses the relationship among Detroit, the Detroit River, and the Great Lakes.

4 Great Lakes Lore Maritime Museum

367 N 3rd St, Rogers City 49779; (989) 734-0706
http://gllmm.com/

This is a hall of fame for the working people who have served the shipping industry. The museum honors its inductees with a ceremony and a collage that features their pictures, their history, and the ships on which they sailed. The museum also features a collection of artifacts, displays about American Indians, fur traders, lighthouse keepers, and life saving stations. There are also model ships, photographs, and illustrations of lighthouses, docks, warehouses, and shipping offices. If you visit, consider a trip in August, when the museum celebrates its inductees, allowing a very personal look at the Great Lakes sailors.

5 Great Lakes Maritime Center

51 Water St, Port Huron; (810) 985-8287
http://greatlakesmaritimecenter.com/

The Great Lakes Maritime Center is a great vantage point for ship watching, but it's also a place to learn about the history of shipping. Inside, videos and displays tell the story, but if you want to learn more, you can also time your visit to coincide with visits by experts. At the center, you can also check out the world headquarters of BoatNerd.com (the premiere website about Great Lakes shipping), where you can get all your boat-related questions answered. After you've spent some time indoors, go outside to the walkway and ship-watch with your binoculars.

6 Great Lakes Naval Memorial and Museum

1346 Bluff St, Muskegon; (231) 755-1230
www.silversidesmuseum.org/index.htm

A real submarine from World War II and a Coast Guard cutter from the Prohibition era are anchored at the dock and waiting for you to get onboard. Here is a chance to step onto (and into) a submarine— and if you don't leave it with admiration for the men who survived in these conditions, we will be amazed. The USS *Silversides* was commissioned eight days after Pearl Harbor and was called The Lucky Boat, as it sunk an astonishing 23 ships and damaged another 14. The sub was eventually declared a National Historic Landmark. The other boat here is a Coast Guard cutter, and it saw another form of action: during Prohibition, it patrolled the Great Lakes, a major route for the transportation of illegal liquor. If the exhibits, displays and boat tours don't wear you out, you can add a movie to your day and learn more about the Navy's role in war.

7 Great Lakes Shipwreck Museum

Great Lakes Shipwreck Museum—Whitefish Point, 18335 N Whitefish Point Rd, Paradise 49768; (888) 492-3747
www.shipwreckmuseum.com/

Located on the premises of the Whitefish Point Light Station and next door to the Whitefish Point Bird Observatory, this destination will definitely require a day to explore. Gordon Lightfoot's "The Wreck of the *Edmund Fitzgerald*" is probably the most famous song about the Great Lakes, and if that song still lingers in your mind and you want to know what happened, this is the place to find out. Sunk in a narrow neck between Lake Michigan and Lake Ontario during a terrible November gale, the story of the *Edmund Fitzgerald* is told in detail here, along with the stories of many other wrecks. There are artifacts, recovered relics, videos, a collection of models, and displays that tell these haunting, but important, stories.

8 Michigan Maritime Museum

260 Dyckman Ave, South Haven; (269) 637-8078
www.michiganmaritimemuseum.org/

Appropriately located on the shore of Lake Michigan, this museum highlights Michigan's maritime heritage on the Great Lakes. The exhibits here vary, but all are inspiring and informative, and there's also a research library. There are more hands-on activities, too; there is a center where visitors can sign up for boat building classes or classes pertaining to other maritime skills. Whatever you do, visit often, as there are many special events and speakers, and the events often feature costumes and dramatic reenactments. Also, if you go down to the water, be sure to check out the sloop, *Friends Good Will*, and the river launch, *Lindy Lou*.

9 Michigan Underwater Preserves

Michigan Underwater Preserve Council Inc, 560 N State St, St. Ignace 49781; (906) 643-8717
www.michiganpreserves.org/

Each of the Great Lakes has a long history of shipwrecks, and Michigan alone has countless shipwrecks. Certain parts of the lake are more dangerous, and wrecks are often concentrated there, making such sites worthy of a special trip. In Michigan, more than 12 distinct underwater preserves have been established to protect these historic sites, and today these preserves cover more than 2,300 square miles of the Great Lakes. Of course, visiting these areas can be dangerous, so you need be very well prepared before visiting them. In addition, if you visit, remember that these are historic sites, so it goes without saying that you shouldn't take anything from these sites. Show the wrecks (and future divers) the respect they deserve.

10 Museum Ship Valley Camp

Corner of Johnston & Water, Sault Ste. Marie
www.saulthistoricsites.com/museum-ship-valley-camp-3/

The SS *Valley Camp* was a lake freighter before she became a museum. The ship offers tours of her deck and her cargo holds. If you can take your eyes off the ship itself, the interior of the ship is a museum with more than 20,000 square feet of space and more than 100 exhibits, including access to the crew quarters and the captain's quarters. The museum includes two lifeboats from the *Edmund Fitzgerald*; these tore away during the sinking and were never used by the crew. You can also watch a video about the infamous 1975 storm in which the great boat sunk.

11 Pictured Rocks Cruises

100 City Park Dr, Munising 49862; (906) 387-2379
www.picturedrocks.com/

One of the best ways to see the Pictured Rocks National Lakeshore is by boat. These boats are small enough to enable visitors to get a good look at the Pictured Rocks, but you're sheltered if Lake Superior acts up. On the ride out of the harbor, the staff will share stories of shipwrecks and lighthouses. Once you're out of the bay, visitors will ooh and aah at the wave-washed sandstone cliffs that are replete with colorful patterns and sculpted caves and bays. On these tours, there is plenty of time to take photos, and the captain navigates the waters with precision, enabling a close look. Try taking the ride at different times of day to see how light can change the view. When you're done, enter the park itself and see the cliffs from above.

12 Soo Locks Boat Tours

PO Box 739, Sault Ste. Marie 49783; Dock #1, 1157 E Portage Ave, Dock #2, 515 E Portage Ave; (800) 432-6301, (906) 632-6301
www.soolocks.com/index.phtml

A boat tour through the Soo Locks is the perfect way to gain perspective on the engineering feat of the locks. These tours take place on the St. Marys River, the short river that connects Lake Superior with Lake Huron and the remaining Great Lakes. All vessels going to or from Lake Superior have to pass through this bottleneck, and that makes these locks internationally significant. In all, the tour covers 4 U.S. locks, St. Marys Rapids, giant hydroelectric plants, and a historic Canadian lock. In the process, you'll see a variety of boats and you can learn about the freighters and "salties" that pass through. There are a number of other exciting cruise options, too. You can choose a dinner cruise, a sunset cruise or a lighthouse cruise.

13 Soo Locks Visitor Center and Observation Area

312 W Portage Ave, Sault Ste. Marie 49783; Vessel Hotline (906) 253-9290
www.lre.usace.army.mil/where/behindthecastle/exhibitcenters/soolocksvisitor-center/

Twenty-one feet may not seem like much, but that's the difference between the elevation of Lake Superior and Lake Huron. To enable ships to move from lake to lake, locks were needed. The first locks on the U.S. side were built in 1855, and they soon became some of the largest and busiest locks in the world. The newest lock was built in 1968 to accommodate the giants of the Great Lakes fleet.

Why visit? This is one of the best places in the world to see working ships up close. The two locks (MacArthur and Poe) handle 10,000 vessel passages per year, but traffic can fluctuate. It is a good idea to call the hotline the day you plan to visit. A visitor center includes all sorts of information about the various locks that have existed here. Better yet, the center includes a sheltered observation platform, so you can relax and watch the big ships pass by.

14 Star of Saugatuck Boat Cruises

716 Water St, PO Box 654; Saugatuck 49453; (269) 857-4261
http://saugatuckboatcruises.com/

Forget the tall ships and ore ships and go back in time onboard a ship that Mark Twain was familiar with: the paddlewheeler. As the paddlewheels turn, they create a nice rhythm, enabling visitors to relax and see the city from a new angle. During the day, you can watch the bustling activity around you, and in the evening you can go for a sunset cruise on Lake Michigan. The upriver tour follows the Kalamazoo River to Lake Kalamazoo and then comes back downstream. Continuing downriver, you can see where the wreck of the *Singapore* lies beneath a sandy shoal. If the weather on Lake Michigan is good, you can even admire some of the region's fascinating lighthouses (including Holland's "Big Red") from the deck of a paddlewheeler.

15 Superior Odyssey

Ellwood A Mattson Lower Harbor Park, Marquette; (906) 361-3668
www.superiorodyssey.com/charterinfo.html

Come onboard the *Coaster II*, a historic wooden-hulled gaff schooner with topsails, and let the wind take you along the rugged Lake Superior coast. Setting out from the Marquette harbor, there are a variety of sailing options. There are 2-hour-long trips (daylight or sunset), 4-hour-long trips to Presque Isle, and 8-hour trips to Partridge Island. Overnight trips, themed events and parties are available, too. No matter which trip you choose, Captain Economides will entertain you while providing a sailing experience you won't forget.

16 Thunder Bay National Marine Sanctuary at the Great Lakes Maritime Heritage Center

500 W Fletcher St, Alpena; (989) 356-8805
http://thunderbay.noaa.gov/

The Thunder Bay National Marine Sanctuary is one of only 14 national marine sanctuaries, and the only one in the world in freshwater. It preserves nearly 200 historic shipwrecks in and around Thunder Bay. Located on Lake Huron, many of these shipwrecks are intact; they range in depth from a few inches to more than 200 feet. If you are interested in the history of shipwrecks, this is the place for you. The displays here are filled with hands-on exhibits and stunning visuals. You can even climb aboard a life-size replica of a wooden schooner! Many recreational opportunities exist in sanctuary waters, including a glass bottom boat, kayaking, snorkeling and scuba diving. If you have the time and interest, consider visiting the Thunder Bay Sanctuary Research Collection, one of the largest archival collections of Great Lakes maritime history, located at the Alpena County George N. Fletcher Public Library.

17 Traverse City Tall Ship

Traverse Tall Ship Company, 13258 SW Bay Shore Dr, Traverse City 49684;
(231) 941-2000, (800) 678-0383
www.tallshipsailing.com/

Traverse City is home to wineries, bike trails and quaint shops, but it is also home to the 114-foot-long, 59-passenger schooner *Manitou*, which offers 3 different cruises every day of the week. On these 2-hour-long cruises, this elegant sailing vessel plies the scenic Grant Traverse Bay of Lake Michigan. There are a few surprising cruise options. For example, you might want to try a Moomers Ice Cream sail, or a sail that features local microbrews and pizza. If you prefer wine, another cruise focuses on local wines, and if you love fine cuisine, try the food made by Silver Swan Homemade Foods. And if you really want a full experience, sign up for a night on The Floating Bed and Breakfast option. Those looking for a true adventure can take a 4-day cruise to the islands, bays and coastal villages of northern Lake Michigan.

Tahquamenon Falls

The physics of waterfalls are not hard to explain: water flows down a stream, the bedrock determines whether the river is flat or has falls, and gravity moves the water downhill and downstream. But that description doesn't explain the magic of falling water. If you like waterfalls, come to Michigan, as its U.P. is home to more than 200 named falls.

WATERFALLS

1 Agate Falls

Joseph E. Oravec Roadside Park, Trout Creek 49947-9722; (906) 353-6558
www.dnr.state.mi.us/parksandtrails/Details.aspx?id=413&type=SPRK

An easy waterfall to see on the Ontonagon River, Agate Falls is located at a scenic rest area. The view from the bottom of the falls is really outstanding, and the river itself is 80 feet wide and forested. A hiking bridge, which once carried a Duluth, South Shore and Atlantic Railway right-of-way, spans the falls. If you want to have a picnic lunch, the rest area has tables. One note of warning: the trail to the falls is steep and can be slippery.

2 Alger Falls

1 mile south of Munising
www.munising.org/waterfalls.php

This is an easy falls to get to. Located 1 mile south of Munising and just a few yards from M-28, if you leave your car, you can find a bit of solitude here. (You can also observe it from your vehicle.) Note that the water level of this falls can drop quickly and dramatically, so check the weather in advance.

3 Black River Falls

8 miles south of Ishpeming

Dropping 20–30 feet through a narrow rock channel, this falls churns and foams more than most Michigan waterfalls. The falls are a quick hike along a scenic path bordered by impressive pine trees. The waterfalls can be viewed from an island at the center of the river, which is easy to reach, thanks to a footbridge.

4 Black River Scenic Byway

Ottawa National Forest; (906) 932-1330
http://byways.org/explore/byways/10780/

The Black River has many great waterfalls that are beautiful and firsthand looks at Michigan's geology. This scenic byway will take you to trails you can use to explore a number of them. The 20-foot

Great Conglomerate Falls is a recommended destination and is named for the unique conglomerate rock that forms the base of the falls. Conglomerate is a rock that contains other small rocks. Other notable waterfalls on the byway include Gorge Falls (25 feet), Potawatomi Falls (30 feet), Sandstone Falls (15 feet), Rainbow Falls (30 feet), and Gabbro Falls (40 feet).

5 Bond Falls

Bond Falls Scenic Site, Bond Falls Rd, Paulding 49969; (906) 353-6558
www.michigandnr.com/parksandtrails/Details.aspx?id=412&type=SPRK

As there are so many beautiful waterfalls in Michigan, it is hard to dub any waterfall as the "best" in the U.P., but many consider Bond Falls at the top of the list. Bond Falls is on the middle branch of the Ontonagon River and tumbles over a thick belt of fractured rock, with a drop of 40 feet. The falls are quite accessible, too. There is roadside parking, picnic tables near the top of the falls, and an accessible boardwalk with six viewing locations.

6 Canyon Falls

7 miles south of L'Anse on US 41; L'Anse 49946; (800) 743-4908
www.dnr.state.mi.us/publications/pdfs/wildlife/viewingguide/up/15Canyon/index.htm

Thanks to a convenient boardwalk that leads through a cedar swamp, you can get a great view of the 15-foot Canyon Falls on the Sturgeon River. As you walk downstream, the name for the falls will become apparent. The trails are not maintained downstream and you need to be cautious, but it is well worth the effort; nearby you can even go further afield in the Sturgeon River Gorge Wilderness Area of the Ottawa National Forest. Note that the parking lot is not plowed in the winter, but during the other seasons there is even a restroom provided for you.

7 Manabezho Falls

33303 Headquarters Rd, Ontonagon 49953-9087
www.michigandnr.com/parksandtrails/Details.aspx?type=SPRK&id=426
www.michigan.gov/dnr/0,1607,7-153-30301_31154_31260-54025--,00.html

On the west side of Porcupine Mountains Wilderness Park, the Presque Isle River comes to a spectacular end that features shoots, rapids, falls and an island that can be reached by a footbridge. Manabezho Falls is the largest waterfall on this spectacular last mile of the river. In addition to the scenery, there is also a large campground, restrooms, picnic facilities, trails and everything you need to have a wonderful day.

8 Munising Falls

Munising Falls Visitor Center (summer only), 1505 Sand Point Rd, Munising 49862; (906) 387-4310
www.nps.gov/piro/planyourvisit/waterfalls.htm

Little Munising Creek has a spectacular ending. It falls 50 feet over a lip of sandstone and past a crescent-shaped rock cliff that has been eroded by years of water flow. Even better, thanks to a well-constructed boardwalk, this waterfall is as easy to access as it is beautiful. Nearby there is an interpretive center (summer only), ample parking and occasional park ranger interpretive programs. And because the falls are so easy to access, we recommend a winter visit, when an ice column extends for the height of the falls.

9 Sable Falls—Pictured Rocks National Lakeshore

About 1 mile west of Grand Marais on Alger Co Rd H-58
www.nps.gov/piro/planyourvisit/waterfalls.htm

On the east border of Pictured Rocks National Lakeshore, this waterfall is located in a deep valley. Even though the falls are relatively small, they are still dramatic, as the water moves past big boulders and follows a natural stairway to the lake. You can approach the falls from the national park trail and stairs that start inland, or walk from Grand Marais to the mouth and follow the trail up to the falls.

10 Spray Falls and Bridalveil Falls

Pictured Rocks National Lakeshore, PO Box 40, Munising 49862-0040
Interagency Visitor Center (year-round), 400 E Munising Ave, Munising 49862; (906) 387-3700
www.nps.gov/piro/planyourvisit/waterfalls.htm
Pictured Rocks Cruises, 100 City Park Dr, Munising 49862; (906) 387-2379
www.picturedrocks.com/

These magnificent waterfalls originate as small streams that run through Pictured Rocks National Lakeshore and exit from the top of the cliffs straight into the lake. Spray Falls is a free-fall waterfall, while Bridalveil Falls flows down a sloping cliff face. Bridalveil is a seasonal waterfall that slows to a trickle in the summer and fall.

These are some of the most dramatic waterfalls in Michigan because of the spectacular surroundings. They are best viewed from one of several vantage points. The Pictured Rocks boat tours take you out for a wonderful lakeside view that captures the grandeur of the panorama; sea kayaks get you in close and even wet (but be careful because rocks can accompany the water), and a wilderness hike will give you a variety of looks at the falls. Check the weather because the view is best after a good rain.

11 Tahquamenon State Park

41382 W M 123, Paradise 49768; (906) 492-3415
www.michigandnr.com/parksandtrails/Details.aspx?id=428&type=SPRK

This park encompasses almost 50,000 acres of wild beauty and provides access to the magnificent Tahquamenon Falls and Lower Falls. In terms of volume, Tahquamenon is the third-largest falls east of the Mississippi River. Lower Falls consists of a series of 5 drops that cascade around an island. The large falls is 200 feet wide and 48 feet high with an estimated 50,000 gallons of water per second flowing through. Steps lead down to the falls, and there is a fully accessible trail and many places to get pictures of the canyon and falls.

12 Yellow Dog Falls

Yellow Dog (Hills) Falls, Co Rd 510, Marquette 49855
www.travelmarquettemichigan.com/recreation/waterfalls/

Yellow Dog Falls is approximately 50 feet wide with a vertical drop of 30 feet. One unique and distinctive feature that photographers enjoy is a huge boulder that sits in the center of the falls and splits the flow. The overall drop of the falls is 20 feet and part of a series of rapids and drops. To get here you must drive out of town and find the hiking trail on the south side of the river that is approximately a half-mile downstream. The walking trail is in good condition, but it includes roots and rocks and approaches the falls from the top.

Waterfalls

ENJOYING THE SNOW

Downhill Skiing

Alpine Valley Ski Area
6775 E Highland Rd, White Lake 48383; Business Office (248) 887-2180
www.skialpinevalley.com/

Big Powderhorn Mountain
Big Powderhorn Mountain Resort; N11375 Powderhorn Rd, Bessemer 49911;
(800) 501-7669, (906) 935-4838
www.bigpowderhorn.net/

Bittersweet Ski Area
600 River Rd, Otsego 49078; Business Office (269) 694-2820
www.skibittersweet.com/pages/home.cfm?CFID=1614138&CFTOKEN=48681253

Boyne Ski Mountains
Boyne Highlands, 600 Highland Dr, Harbor Springs 49740; (231) 526-3000
www.boyne.com/Winter/Two_Mountains/index.html

Boyne Mountain, One Boyne Mountain Rd, Boyne Falls 49713; (231) 549-6000

Crystal Mountain
12500 Crystal Mountain Dr, Thompsonville 49683-9742; (231) 378-2000
www.crystalmountain.com/

Hickory Hills Ski Area
2000 Randolph St, Traverse City 49684; (231) 947-8566
Contact year-round: 625 Woodmere Ave, Traverse City 49686; (231) 922-4910
www.ci.traverse-city.mi.us/parks-recreation-department/hickory-hills-ski-area

Indianhead Mountain
500 Indianhead Rd, Wakefield 49968; (800) 3-INDIAN, (800) 346-3426
www.indianheadmtn.com/

Mt. Brighton
Mt. Brighton Ski Resort, 4141 Bauer Rd, Brighton 48116
www.mtbrighton.com/

Nub's Nob Ski Resort
500 Nubs Nob Rd, Harbor Springs; (231) 526-2131
http://nubsnob.com/

Snowboarding

Hawk Island & Snow Park
Hawk Island Park, 1601 E Cavanaugh St, Lansing 48910
http://pk.ingham.org/ParksTrails/HawkIsland.aspx

Marquette Mountain
4501 M-553, Marquette 49855; (800) 944-SNOW, (800) 944-7669
(906) 225-1155
www.marquettemountain.com/home.php

Powderhorn Mountain
N11375 Powderhorn Rd, Bessemer 49911; (800) 501-SNOW, (800) 501-7669,
(906) 932-4838
www.bigpowderhorn.net/

Shanty Creek
5780 Shanty Creek Rd, Bellaire 49615; (800) 678-4111
www.shantycreek.com/winter/

Ski Brule
397 Brule Mountain Rd, Iron River 49935; (800) DO-BRULE, (800) 362-7853
http://skibrule.com/

Snowmobile Trails

Snowmobile Trails
For trails: www.trailreport.com/
www.fishweb.com/recreation/snowmobile/trails/index.html

For maps:
www.michigan.gov/dnr/0,1607,7-153-10366_34947-31074--,00.html

Cross-Country Skiing

ABR Ski Trails
E5299 W Pioneer Rd, Ironwood 49938; (906)-932-3502 (do not call after 9 p.m.)
www.abrski.com/skiing

Black Mountain Pathway
Co Rd 489, Onaway 49765; (989) 785-4251
www.michigandnr.com/parksandtrails/details.aspx?id=50&type=SFPW

Blueberry Ridge Pathway
Co Rd 553 & Co Rd 480, Escanaba River State Forest, Marquette 49855
www.michigandnr.com/parksandtrails/Details.aspx?id=88&type=SFPW

Corsair Ski Trails
3 miles south of River Rd on Monument Rd, Oscoda
www.n-sport.com/CrossCountrySkiing.html; www.oscoda.com/snowmobile.php

MTU Trails, Michigan Tech Nordic Training Center
1400 Townsend Dr, Houghton 49931-1295
www.sportsrec.mtu.edu/index.php?option=com_content&view=article&id=81&-
Itemid=65

Noquemenon Trail Network
PO Box 746, Marquette 49855; (906) 235-6861
www.noquetrails.org/

Rapid River National Ski Trail
Hiawatha National Forest
From the intersection of US 2 & US 41 in Rapid River, drive 6 miles north on US 41 to the trailhead; trailhead will be on the left (west) side of the highway

Sand Dunes Ski Trail
Located near Lake Michigan, south of Hwy. 2 and west of Brevort Lake Road

Swedetown Trails
Copper Island Cross Country Ski Club, PO Box 214, Calumet 49913; (906) 337-1170
www.swedetowntrails.org/

Valley Spur Ski Trail
Hiawatha National Forest, I-94, approximately 5 miles from Munising
www.valleyspur.org/

Wolverine Nordic Trails
5851 Sunset Rd, Ironwood 49938; (906) 932-0347
www.wolverinenordic.com/index.html

Tobogganing, Skating, Luge & More

Al Quaal Recreation Area
501 Poplar St, Ishpeming 49849; (906) 486-6181
www.ishpemingcity.org/departments/parks-and-recreation/al-quaal-recreation-area

Echo Valley Winter Sports Park
8495 E H Ave, Kalamazoo 49004; (616) 349-3291

Muskegon Winter Sports Complex
Muskegon Luge, 462 Scenic Dr N, Muskegon 49445
www.msports.org/

U.S. National Ski and Snowboard Hall of Fame
610 Palms Ave, PO Box 191, Ishpeming; (906) 485-6323
www.skihall.com/

Ski Flying

Copper Peak Ski Flying
Copper Peak Inc, PO Box 159, Ironwood 49938; (906) 932-3500
www.copperpeak.org/

FESTIVALS

Nature and Science

Ann Arbor Earth Day Festival
Leslie Science & Nature Center, 1831 Traver Rd, Ann Arbor 48105
www.LeslieSNC.org/; www.a2gov.org/government/publicservices/fieldopera-
tions/solidwasteunit/education/Pages/EarthDayFestival.aspx

Brown Trout Festival
Alpena
www.alpenami-browntrout.com/

Green Street Fair
Plymouth
First weekend in May since 2007
www.greenstreetfair.com/index.htm

Keweenaw Migratory Bird Festival
Copper Harbor
www.keweenawimbd.org/festival.html

National Cherry Festival
Held in July in Traverse City
www.cherryfestival.org/

Tulip Time Festival
74 W 8th St, Holland 49423; (800) 822-2770, (616) 396-4221
www.tuliptime.com/

Winter Festivals

Hunter Ice Festival
Niles
http://huntericefestival.org/

Ice Sculpture Spectacular
350 S Main St, Plymouth 48170
http://plymouthicefestival.org/

MTU Winter Carnival
Houghton
www.mtu.edu/carnival/

North American Snow Festival
(800) 22-LAKES, (800) 225-2537, (231) 775-0657
www.cadillacmichigan.com/pages.php?tabid=21&pageid=131&title=Snow+
Fest+-+NASF

Culture and Heritage

African World Festival
Charles H. Wright Museum of African American History, 315 E Warren Ave, Detroit 48201; (313) 494-5800, Fax (313) 494-5855
www.thewright.org/african-world-festival

Alpena Blues Festival
Alpena Blues Coalition, PO Box 874, Alpena 49707
www.alpenablues.com/

Ann Arbor Top of the Park
310 Depot St, Ste 3, Ann Arbor 48104; (734) 994-5999
www.annarborsummerfestival.org/index.php/events/top_of_the_park/

FestiFools
University of Michigan, Ann Arbor 48109
http://festifools.org/

Frankenmuth, the City of Festivals
Frankenmuth; (800) FUN-TOWN, (800) 386-8696
www.frankenmuthfestivals.com/

The Flint Greek Festival
E Baldwin Rd, Grand Blanc
http://flintgreekfestival.com/

Greek Independence Day Parade
Detroit
http://detroit.greekparades.com/index.htm

Kalamazoo Greek Festival
http://kalamazoogreekfest.com/

Heikinpaiva Finnish Festival
www.americantowns.com/mi/hancock/news/heikinpaiva-finnish-american-mid-winter-festival-2011-2901070
http://pasty.com/heikki/sched.html

Irish Festival
Clare
http://clearlyclaremi.com/irish/festival/

Jackson Storyfest
Jackson; (517) 499-2290
http://jacksonstoryfest.org/

Michigan Kite Festivals
Great Lakes Kite Festival
www.mackite.com/glskc.htm

Parade of Nations and International Food Festival

Houghton
www.doe.mtu.edu/international/international_festival.html

Polish Festival

PO Box 53, Bronson 49028
www.bronson-mi.com/polish-festival

St. Demetrios Greek Orthodox Church

4970 Mackinaw at McCarty, Saginaw 48603
www.stdemetrios.mi.goarch.org/

St. George Church

Bloomfield Hills
http://stgeorge-bh.org//

St. Nicholas Greek Orthodox Church

3109 Scio Church Rd, Ann Arbor 48103
www.stnickaa.org/

St. Nicholas Greek Orthodox Church

Troy 48098
http://opafest.com/

Scottish Heritage

Alma
www.almahighlandfestival.com/

Ypsilanti Heritage Fest

Ypsilanti
www.ypsilantiheritagefestival.com/

ORCHARDS & VINEYARDS

Apples

Annual Charlevoix Apple Fest
Charlevoix; (231) 547-2101
www.charlevoix.org

Art & Apples Festival
Rochester; (248) 651-4110
www.ArtandApples.com

Bangor Harvest Festival
Bangor; (269) 655-5000
www.ci.bangor.mi.us/

Coldwater Applefest
Coldwater; (517) 279-6903
www.coldwaterdda.org

Four Flags Area Apple Festival
Niles; (269) 683-8870
http://fourflagsapplefestival.org

Michigan Apple Festival
Charlotte
www.michiganapplefestival.com/

Michigan Apple Tours
www.michiganappletours.com/

Tecumseh's 19th Annual Appleumpkin Festival
Tecumseh; (517) 424-6003;
www.downtowntecumseh.com

Blueberries

Blueberry Festival in Otter Lake
www.blueberrylanefarms.com/

Blueberry Lane Farms
13240 Blueberry Ln, Otter Lake 48464; 810 793-4590

Marquette Blueberry Festival
http://downtownmarquette.org/blueberryfestival.php

Montrose Blueberry Festival in Montrose
PO Box 316, Montrose 48457-0316;
(810) 639-3475
http://montroseblueberryfestival.net/

National Blueberry Festival in South Haven
www.blueberryfestival.com/

Paradise Blueberry Festival in Paradise
(906) 492-3219
www.exploringthenorth.com/blue/berry.html

Cherries

National Cherry Festival
Held in July in Traverse City
www.cherryfestival.org/

Michigan Wine Trails

Lake Michigan Shore Wine Trail
www.lakemichiganshorewinetrail.com/

Leelanau Wine Trail
http://lpwines.com/wine-trail-map/

Pick Your Own

A variety of pick your own options are available at: www.pickyourown.org/MI.htm

Pumpkins

Davison Pumpkin Festival
Zeeland Chamber of Commerce, 149 Main Pl, Zeeland 49464; (616) 772-2494
www.davisonpumpkinfestival.com/

Tuscola Pumpkin Fest
157 N State St, Caro 48723; (989) 673-2511
www.tuscolapumpkinfest.com/

Strawberries

Alden Strawberry Festival
Alden
http://visitalden.com/eventsinalden/strawberryfestival.html

Copper Country Strawberry Festival
Chassell
www.coppercountrystrawberryfestival.com/

National Strawberry Festival
Bellevue; (313) 383-8920
www.nationalstrawberryfest.com/

SPORTS

Baseball

Detroit Tigers—Comerica Park
2100 Woodward Ave, Detroit 48201-3470; (313) 962-4000
http://detroit.tigers.mlb.com/det/ballpark/index.jsp

The Great Lakes Loons
Dow Diamond, 825 E Main St, Midland 48640; (989) 837-2255
www.milb.com/index.jsp?sid=t456

Lansing Lugnuts Professional Baseball
505 E Michigan Ave, Lansing 48912; (517) 485-4500
www.lansinglugnuts.com

Wuerfel Park—Traverse City Beach Bums
Wuerfel Park—Traverse City Beach Bums, 333 Stadium Dr, Traverse City 49684;
(231) 943-0100
www.traversecitybeachbums.com/

Basketball

Detroit Pistons—The Palace
Palace Sports & Entertainment, 6 Championship Dr, Auburn Hills 48326;
(248) 377-0100
www.nba.com/pistons/

Football

Detroit Lions—Ford Field
2000 Brush St, Detroit 48226; (313) 262-2012
www.detroitlions.com/index.html

Hockey

Detroit Red Wings
Joe Louis Arena, W Jefferson and the Riverfront; (313) 396-7575
http://redwings.nhl.com/

Saginaw Spirit—Ontario Hockey League
Saginaw Spirit Hockey Club, Dow Center Arena, PO Box 6157, Saginaw 48608;
(989) 497-7747
www.saginawspirit.com

Collegiate

Michigan State University Athletics
248 Jenison Field House, East Lansing 48824; (517) 355-1610
www.msuspartans.com

Northern Michigan Hockey and Olympic Training Center
1401 Presque Isle Ave, Marquette 49855-5301; 906-227-1000
www.nmu.edu/sportsrecsports/node/5
www.nmu.edu/sportsusoec/node/297

University of Michigan
1000 S State St, Ann Arbor 48109-2201
www.mgoblue.com/

Index

About the Author

Mike Link is the retired director of the Audubon Center of the North Woods in Sandstone, MN. He is also the author of 22 books, and an adjunct professor at Hamline University, speaker and wilderness guide. His life has been in the environment since 1966 when he began writing a weekly column called Link's Lore and he continues to speak on behalf of the planet in his many roles. He and his wife, Kate Crowley, walked around Lake Superior's shore in 2010, the only couple to ever do so, and they plan to bike the length of the Mississippi River next. They are travelers who love to explore the world, meet people, and challenge themselves to stay active.

Mike has received awards in Environmental Education from the Izaak Walton League, the National Association of Interpretation and the North American Association of Environmental Education. He is the first recipient of the Lifetime Achievement Award from the Minnesota Association of Environmental Education and he and Kate received awards from the Binational Forum and *Lake Superior Magazine.*

As grandparents, he and Kate have enjoyed the opportunity to travel and explore with their grandchildren and authored the *Grandparents* series for Adventure Publications. They love to challenge their grandchildren to explore and enjoy nature, to learn, and to be open to new opportunities. The five grandchildren have been the source of inspiration for their walk, their work, and their plans. It is their desire to leave a better planet for their grandchildren and to inspire others to do the same.

Michigan Day Trips is a reflection of the broad interests and the love of travel that defines Mike. He asks you to have fun, be good to others, and care for the only planet we will ever have.